how to
keep
house
while
drowning

how to keep house *while* drowning

a gentle approach to cleaning and organizing

KC Davis

Simon Element

New York   London   Toronto   Sydney   New Delhi

SIMON
ELEMENT

An Imprint of Simon & Schuster, Inc.
1230 Avenue of the Americas
New York, NY 10020

First Simon Element hardcover edition May 2022

SIMON ELEMENT is a trademark of Simon & Schuster, Inc.

For information about special discounts for bulk purchases,
please contact Simon & Schuster Special Sales at 1-866-506-1949
or business@simonandschuster.com.

The Simon & Schuster Speakers Bureau can bring authors to your
live event. For more information or to book an event,
contact the Simon & Schuster Speakers Bureau at 1-866-248-3049
or visit our website at www.simonspeakers.com.

Interior design by Jennifer Chung

Illustrations by Lydia Ellen Greaves

Happy icon by Austin Condiff/The Noun Project

Manufactured in the United States of America

7 9 10 8 6

Library of Congress Cataloging-in-Publication Data has been applied for.

ISBN 978-1-6680-0284-1
ISBN 978-1-6680-0285-8 (ebook)

This book is dedicated to my family.

contents

how to read this book

this book has been designed for maximum accessibility for readers who are neurodivergent. Words are printed in a sans serif font and left angled to make reading the text easier. Paragraphs and chapters are short and main points are bolded to account for both attention and comprehension needs, and literal interpretations are offered of any metaphors used for clarity.

I have written this book to be comprehensive without being too long or intimidating. However, if you feel you do not have the capacity to read the whole book right now, please follow my shortcut journey through the book. This abridged way of reading the book should only take you thirty minutes to one hour depending on your reading speed. Begin with the first page.

introduction

In February 2020 I had my second baby. Having struggled with postpartum anxiety in a previous pregnancy and knowing that my husband's new job was going to have him working seven days a week, I set up a comprehensive postpartum support plan for myself. My toddler would go to preschool four days a week, family would rotate in every week for the first two months, a cleaning service would come in once a month, and the new moms group I had helped form would drop off food and stop by to offer a hand. I was so proud of my plan—and it ended before it even began. Three weeks after I gave birth, covid lockdowns were announced and the entire thing collapsed overnight.

The world got very small. Very fast. Days rolled into each other in a sleepless strand of breastfeeding difficulties, toddler melt-downs, and, soon, depression. Numb and overwhelmed by the isolation, I watched my house crumble around me. I tried every day

to figure out how to take care of both babies' needs at once, and I went to bed every night haunted by my failure. As I lay in bed I dared to think things I was too frightened to say out loud: "What if I have made a huge mistake? Maybe I am only capable of being a good mom to one kid. Maybe I'm not cut out for caring for two. I don't understand how anyone does this. I am failing them." One day my sister began sending me funny TikTok videos. "You have to get on this video app. I feel like it would cheer you up to laugh." I relented and even got the courage one day to make a post of my own: a video making light of the house turned disaster we had been living in. To the background of a viral audio that sang about all the shit that wasn't going to get done that day, I showed shots of my messy living room, my overflowing sink, and the enchilada pan I had left to fend for itself for three days. "No pipe dreams here!" I quipped in the description, tacking on the hashtag #breastfeeding. Surely, from the annals of the internet, moms everywhere would rally to chuckle in solidarity at how hard it is to have a newborn baby. Instead, I got this comment:

There it was. The word that had haunted me for so much of my life. As I was a messy and creative woman with undiagnosed ADHD, that word held a deep and cutting power. Like a snake, I felt the voice that visited me nightly crawl up my throat, wrap its body around my neck, and hiss into my ear, "See? I told you you were failing." My professional experience as a therapist had shown me time and time again that being overwhelmed is not a personal failure, but as most of you may know, the gulf between what we know in our minds and what we feel in our hearts is often an insurmountable distance. In that moment, I couldn't help but absorb that lie that my inability to keep a clean home was direct evidence of my deep character failing of laziness.

In reality, this could not be further from the truth. I'd birthed a baby with no pain medication after meticulous research and planning; I'd pumped breast milk every three hours to get her through her NICU stay and continued to wake six times a night to breastfeed after bringing her home. I got up every day despite the postpartum depression to care for my newborn and my toddler all day long. I even managed to make homemade enchiladas. And I did all of that while my vagina was literally being held together by stitches.

But to this person on the internet, because my home wasn't clean, I was failing. I was *lazy*.

Were the dishes sky-high and the laundry unfinished? Yes. Did I feel like I was drowning when it came to accomplishing even simple tasks around my home? Absolutely.

I was tired.

I was depressed.

I was overwhelmed.

I was in need of help.

But I was not lazy.

And neither are you.

what are care tasks and
why are they so hard for people?

Care tasks are the "chores" of life: cooking, cleaning, laundry, feeding, dishes, and hygiene. These may seem like noncomplex tasks. **But when you actually break down the amount of time, energy, skill, planning, and maintenance that go into care tasks, they no longer seem simple.** For example, the care task of feeding yourself involves more than just putting food into your mouth. You must also make time to figure out the nutritional needs and preferences of everyone you're feeding, plan and execute a shopping trip, decide how you're going to prepare that food and set aside the time to do so, and ensure that mealtimes come at correct intervals. You need energy and skill to plan, execute, and follow through on these steps every day, multiple times a day, and to deal with any barriers related to your relationship with food and weight, or a lack of appetite due to medical or emotional factors. You must have the emotional energy to deal with the feeling of being overwhelmed when you don't know what to cook and the anxiety it can produce to create a kitchen mess. You may also need the skills to multitask while working, dealing with physical pain, or watching over children.

Now let's look at cleaning: an ongoing task made up of hundreds of small skills that must be practiced every day at the right time and manner in order to "keep going on the business of life." First, you must have the executive functioning to deal with sequentially ordering and prioritizing tasks.[1] You must learn which cleaning must be done daily and which can be done on an interval. You must remember those intervals. You must be familiar with cleaning products and remember to purchase them. You must have the physical energy and time to complete these tasks and the mental health to engage in a low-dopamine errand for an extended period of time. You must have the emotional energy and ability to process any sensory discomfort that comes with dealing with any dirty or soiled materials. "Just clean as you go" sounds nice and efficient, but most people don't appreciate the hundreds of skills it takes to operate that way and the thousands of barriers that can interfere with execution.

Health and hygiene are far more complex than "eat healthy and shower." You must possess the social skills to call the doctor and attend appointments. You must have the time and energy to fill prescriptions and, again, the executive functioning to take the medications every day. Even tasks that appear to be secondhand thoughts to most people—brushing your teeth, washing your hair, changing your clothes—can become almost impossible in the face of functional barriers.

In my work as a therapist I have seen hundreds of clients who struggle with these issues, and I am convinced now more than ever of one simple truth: they are not lazy. **In fact, I do not think laziness exists.**

You know what does exist? Executive dysfunction, procrastination, feeling overwhelmed, perfectionism, trauma, amotivation,

---

1   Executive functioning skills include focusing, planning, organizing, following directions, and more.

chronic pain, energy fatigue, depression, lack of skills, lack of support, and differing priorities.

ADHD, autism, depression, traumatic brain injury, and bipolar and anxiety disorders are just some of the conditions that affect executive function, making planning, time management, working memory, and organization more difficult, and tasks with multiple steps intimidating or boring.

There is an old saying that neurons that fire together wire together. It simply means that your brain can start associating feelings with certain experiences. This means that if a person was in an abusive situation either as a child or in a domestic partnership where cleaning or mess was used as punishment or was the subject of abuse then that person is going to have post-traumatic stress around housekeeping and they may avoid it because it triggers their nervous system.

When barriers to functioning make completing care tasks difficult, a person can experience an immense amount of shame. "How can I be failing at something so simple?" they think to themselves. The critical internal dialogue quickly forms a vicious cycle, paralyzing the person even further. They are unlikely to reach out for help with these tasks due to intense fear of judgment and rejection. As shame and isolation increase, mental health plummets. Self-loathing sets in and motivation vanishes. Sadly, this is often compounded by critical and cruel comments that friends and family make. Being labeled as lazy cements the belief that struggling to complete these simple tasks is, at its core, a moral failure.

If you are crying (or wincing internally) right now, this book is for you. You are not lazy or dirty or gross. You are not a failure. You just need nonjudgmental and compassionate help.

slow, quiet, gentle

So how is this book different from other self-help books? For one, I don't have a program; I have a philosophy: You don't exist to serve your space; your space exists to serve you.

Internalizing this belief will help you a) shift your perspective of care tasks from a moral obligation to a functional errand, b) see what changes you actually *want* to make, and c) weave them into your life with minimal effort, relying not on self-loathing but on self-compassion.

I arrived at this philosophy both through my training and work as a therapist and through my own experience of thinking, for decades, that the way I presented myself and my home determined my worthiness as a person. Even when this motivated me to make "positive" or "productive" changes, they didn't solve my dislike of myself—and the "life improvements" didn't stick for long.

As a teenager, I was so ferociously obsessed with being seen as worth saving that I tried to embody the tragically broken drug addict archetype of Nirvana fame. When I was sent to rehab for a year and a half at the age of sixteen, I was able to crawl out of the addiction but found myself just anxious to be thought of as the poster child of a "good client" as a substitute for genuine self-worth. Even a very real experience of religious faith was hijacked by my need to fill this hole. After becoming a missionary and attending seminary, I was quietly ashamed to discover that a majority of my motivation for doing so was again to become a person who was seen as good enough by those around me.

I realized in my late twenties that I'd been playing out the same pattern over and over without realizing it: looking for a role to fill that would finally make me worthy of kindness and love and belonging.

When I viewed getting my life together as a way for trying to atone for the sin of falling apart, I stayed stuck in a shame-fueled cycle of performance, perfectionism, and failure.

The year I spent stuck inside with my kids during the beginning of the pandemic, while painful in many respects, created an opportunity for me to reexamine my relationship with my space. Our feelings of failure after not living up to the newest self-care movement or organizational system stem from fundamental misunderstanding about what kind of journey we are on. There is a big difference between being on a journey of worthiness and being on a journey of care. If you want to adapt the systems you read about because you feel like if you can finally get on top of your housework or have that rainbow-colored bookcase and perfectly matched socks you'll finally be a person worthy of kindness and love and belonging, you are always going to feel inadequate. Because you are never going to find those things that way. More than likely you are going to set up those systems, cosplay like an adult who has their life together, only to have all those new habits fall apart in a matter of days or weeks. What we need here is a paradigm shift on how we look at ourselves and our space.

I'll say it again: you don't exist to serve your space; your space exists to serve you.

In this book, I'm going to help you find *your* way of keeping a functional home—whatever "functional" means for you. Together, we are going to build a foundation of self-compassion and learn how to stop negative self-talk and shame. Then, and only then, can we begin to look into ways to maneuver around our functional barriers. I have so many tips for how to clean a room when you are overwhelmed, how to hack motivation for times when you feel like doing nothing, how to organize without feeling overwhelmed, ideas for getting the dishes and the laundry done on hard days, and lots of creative hacks for working with a body that doesn't always cooperate. And we are going to do it without endless checklists and overwhelming routines.

As you embark on this journey I invite you to remember these words: "slow," "quiet," "gentle." You are already worthy of love and belonging. This is not a journey of worthiness but a journey of care. A journey of learning how we can care for ourselves when we feel like we are drowning.

Because you must know, dear heart, that you are worthy of care whether your house is immaculate or a mess.

chapter 1

care tasks are morally neutral

morality concerns itself with the goodness or badness of your character and the rightness or wrongness of decisions. Lots of decisions are moral decisions, but cleaning your car regularly is not one of them. You can be a fully functioning, fully successful, happy, kind, generous adult and never be very good at cleaning your dishes in a timely manner or have an organized home. How you relate to care tasks—whether you are clean or dirty, messy or tidy, organized or unorganized—has absolutely no bearing on whether you are a good enough person.

When you view care tasks as moral, the motivation for completing them is often shame. When everything is in place, you don't feel like a failure; when it's messy or untidy, you do.

If you are completing care tasks from a motivation of shame, you are probably also relaxing in shame too—because care tasks never end and you view rest as a reward for good boys and girls. So if you ever actually let yourself sit down and rest, you're thinking, "I don't deserve to do this. There is more to do."

This is an incredibly painful way to live. It affects your entire life: your mental health, your relationships, your friendships, your work or schooling, your physical health. It is impossible for the kindness or affirmation of others to penetrate your heart when you are thinking, "If you only knew . . ." But it doesn't have to be this way. In fact, I have very good news for you.

Care tasks are morally neutral. Being good or bad at them has nothing to do with being a good person, parent, man, woman, spouse, friend. Literally nothing. You are not a failure because you can't keep up with laundry. Laundry is morally neutral.

chapter 2

kindness to future you

On the weekends, my husband, Michael, and I take turns getting up early with the kids so the other one can sleep in. Cleaning the kitchen is one of my tasks in our partnership, and I'm pretty renowned for only doing it every few days. Yet the evening before it's Michael's turn to wake up I found myself taking the time to clear the counter, do the dishes, and take out the trash so that it would be easy for him to prepare the girls' breakfast and take care of them in the morning. Michael has never asked or expected this of me; it was simply something I did to make his life easier. I was typically one to not think that far ahead for myself and find myself hand-washing a day-old milk cup at 7:00 am while my kids cried because they were thirsty. Sort of a stressful way to start the day and I guess I didn't want him to have to go through that. One day I had a thought: "I deserve that exact same kindness. I also deserve a functional space for those mornings I'm taking care of our kids." That I could consider nighttime prep as a kindness to morning me changed my entire relationship with care tasks.

Next time you are trying to talk yourself into doing a care task, what would it be like to replace the voice that says, "Ugh, I should really go clean my house right now because it's a disaster," with "It would be such a kindness to future me if I were to get up right now and do _____. That task will allow me to experience comfort, convenience, and pleasure later."

It isn't a hack, really. It's not a formula guaranteed to make you get up. Sometimes you may not get up even with the change in self-talk. But you know what? You weren't getting up when you were being mean to yourself either, so at least you can be nice to yourself. No one ever shamed themselves into better mental health.

chapter 3

for all the
self-help rejects

arie Kondo says to tri-fold your underwear. The admiral swears making your bed will change your life. Rachel Hollis thinks the key to success is washing your face and believing in yourself. Capsule wardrobes! Rainbow-colored organization! Bullet journals! How many of these have we tried? How many did we stick with? If you're like me, the answer is probably none.

Why is it we rarely stick with them?

I've already talked about the role of shame in first motivating, then ultimately demotivating us. But there's more.

1. Any task or habit requiring extreme force of will depletes your ability to exert that type of energy over time. The truth is that human beings can only exert high effort for short periods. As someone in the addiction recovery world, I often think of a phrase we use when someone is attempting to maintain sobriety through sheer force of will. We call it white-knuckling sobriety because it brings to mind a person whose only solution for restraining themselves from drinking is to grip the edge of their chair so tightly their knuckles turn white. And those of us who have been around awhile know no one stays sober long that way. In addiction recovery, as in most of life, success depends not on having strong willpower, but in developing mental and emotional tools to help you experience the world differently.

2. Many self-help gurus overattribute their success to their own hard work without any regard to the physical, mental, or economic privileges they hold. You can see this when a twenty-year-old fitness influencer says, "We all have the same twenty-four hours!" to a single mom of three. The fitness influencer only needed to add effort to see drastic changes in her health and so assumes that's all anyone is missing. The single mom of three, however, is experiencing very different demands and limitations on her time. For her, she needs not only effort but also

childcare, money for exercise classes, and extra time and energy at the end of a day when she has worked nine hours and then spent an additional five caring for kids and cleaning house. You can see this when a thin, white, rich self-help influencer posts "Choose Joy" on her Instagram with a caption that tells us all that joy is a choice. Her belief that the decision to be a positive person was the key to her joyful life reveals she really does not grasp just how much of her success is due to privileges beyond her control. Someone who is affected by serious mental illness or systemic oppression has a lot more standing in the way of a happy life than a simple attitude adjustment.

3. Different people struggle differently—and privilege isn't the only difference. Someone might find a way to meal plan, or exercise, or organize their pantry that revolutionizes their life. But the solutions that work for them are highly dependent on not only their unique barriers but also their strengths, personality, and interests.

For example, when it comes to my home, I have never been able to just "clean as you go." When I try to, I find myself stressed, overwhelmed, and unable to be present with my family. Instead, I rely on dozens of systems I've created that help me keep my home functional (and I still usually have dishes in the sink and clutter on the floor). However, when I sit down to write or to work on my business, everything flows naturally. Sometimes I have to push myself slightly to get over a hurdle, but the hurdles always feel surmountable. I actually have to set a timer to remind me to look at the clock because I will get carried away and lose track of time. I feel creative, energized, and rewarded at the end of the day.

I have a dear friend who runs a similar business, and we often use each other as a sounding board and support each other. She often calls feeling stuck because she knows what she needs to do to grow her business but struggles to get it done. "It seems like you can crank out seven videos for your social media in the time it takes me to do one. It takes me so long to figure out what to say and to get over my self-consciousness."

She also keeps the cleanest house I've ever seen.

One day she said to me, "You know, KC, the way you feel about your business is the way I feel about my home. I can virtually float through my home tidying here, putting something away there, doing a little housework as I see it, all while enjoying my life and keeping a very clean home. It feels natural and takes only a bit of effort. But when I sit down to run my business, certain aspects of what need to be done make me feel paralyzed, unmotivated, and overwhelmed. It takes extreme effort for me to power through, and I usually have to set up lots of external systems and accountability to get it done."

My friend and I are simply strength-oriented and stuck in different ways, with no discernable reason to which we can point. Because of this, my advice for getting things done at work won't help her at all, mostly because it amounts to "Drink a big coffee and just make yourself do it. Then wait around to be inspired about what to do next." And her advice for getting things done around the house is useless to me. (She once told me, "I just light a candle and think about how good it will feel to get some things done around the house." Lol what?)

I suspect that many people doling out productivity advice focus on areas where they're naturally gifted—areas where all they needed was a little push or a couple of tips to get themselves unstuck. Unlike coffee and candles and believing in yourself, the principles in this book can be customized to your unique barriers, strengths, and interests.

chapter 4

gentle skill building: the five things tidying method

When you look at very messy space, it's easy to feel over-whelmed. Take a few minutes to speak some compassionate words to yourself and take a deep breath. **Although it looks like a lot, there are actually only five things in any room: (1) trash, (2) dishes, (3) laundry, (4) things that have a place and are not in their place, and (5) things that do not have a place.**

1. The first step is to take a trash bag and pick up all the trash. Throw it away into the bag. Take large trash items like boxes and stack them together and place the trash bag with it. Do not take the trash out.

2. Next gather all of the dishes and place them in your sink or on your counter. Do not do the dishes.

3. Take a laundry basket and pick up all the clothes and shoes. Place the laundry basket next to the trash pile. Do not do the laundry.

4. Next pick a space in the room like a corner or a desk and put all the items there that have a place back in their place. Then put the items that have no place in a pile. Move to the next space and repeat until all things are back in their spots.

5. Now you will have a pile of things that do not have a place. It will be easier now that the space is clear to tackle this category. You may choose to get rid of some items that have no place and are contributing to clutter. For important things, you can find them a permanent place.

6. Take out your trash to the bin; throw laundry into the wash or laundry room. Now your space is livable. I always save the dishes for another day.

why the five things tidying method works

The Five Things Tidying Method helps the brain know exactly what it is looking for, so instead of seeing a sea of clutter and being paralyzed, it can start to see individual items. Ignoring everything but that one category helps to keep you on track and not get distracted. You can move faster when you know what you are looking for. Trash, laundry, and dishes are being placed into their own containers, so you are not spending lots of time walking around your house putting things away in different places. This makes things get tidier faster. Lastly, completing a category gives you a little dopamine reward. No more spending hours trying to clean and seeing no progress. Our brains need to see progress or they get discouraged. Category cleaning gives your brain multiple, quick finish lines to feel good about.

The categories can be tackled all at once or over a few days. You can choose to do only trash today, only dishes tomorrow, et cetera. You can also institute the timer technique. Decide that you are going to do twenty minutes a day, starting with the categories. Perhaps it takes you three days to get all the trash, but you stick with only trash until it's done. Music, a Netflix show, a podcast, a timer, racing to see how fast you can go, a friend to help you tag team, rewarding yourself with something when you are done—all of these are tools you have to help you.

Lastly, the order of the categories is such that even if you don't finish all the categories, you will be prioritizing removing the items most likely to create health hazards and attract bugs. If you are very overwhelmed, it is an excellent accomplishment to just remove the trash and dishes from your space.

what to do with donations

Listen to me. Picture my hands cupping your face and my eyes looking directly into yours. Take a deep breath. Heed these words: It's okay, friend. Throw it away.

The clothes you've been meaning to donate that have been sitting there for six months—throw them away.

The items you've been planning to sell that have been making your room unfunctional for months—throw them away.

I'm not anti-donation, I'm just pro-realism and pro-accessibility. Today is about getting back to functioning. If you have not done it yet, it's not going to get done. Throw. It. Away. It's okay—really.

chapter 5

gentle self-talk: mess has no inherent meaning

remember that because care tasks are morally neutral, mess has no inherent meaning. When you look at the pile of dishes in the sink and think, "I'm such a failure," that message did not originate from the dishes. Dishes don't think. Dishes don't judge. Dishes cannot make meaning—only people can.

In fact, the meaning assigned to a care task was probably given to you by someone else. Take a moment to think about who it may have been. Your mother? Father? Partner? A grandparent? What messages were you given about domestic care tasks and the meaning behind them? Where did those ideas trickle down from?

I recently saw someone write on social media, "My grand-mother used to say to me, we may be poor but we will be clean. And she would scrub that tiny house until it shone." I'm learning that when marginalized communities face racism or classism, high standards for cleanliness can be a way for a family to re-assert their own dignity in the face of dehumanizing stereotypes about being lazy, unintelligent, or dirty. Loving families might insist that their home sparkle or their children's clothes be spotless, not out of a perceived superiority, but as a way of protecting against discrimination.

There may be other complex and contextual reasons why your family or community gave you the messages they did about care tasks. You may need time to consider, to honor, to grieve, and to process the origins of such messages. In the end, you may decide those messages do not serve you anymore and give mess a new meaning.

Begin to notice how you speak to yourself on days when you feel you have fallen behind. You can set up the best systems in the world and they won't change your life if you still hate yourself on days when you can't keep up. So much of our distress comes not from the unfolded laundry but from the messages we give ourselves. Lazy. Predictable. Unlovable. You do not need to be good at care tasks to learn how to develop a compassionate inner dialogue. You deserve kindness and love regardless of how good you are at care tasks.

You might also be interested in playing back what you tell yourself when you are "succeeding" in care tasks. Do you feel good when your home is clean and laundry is folded? Ask yourself why. It is one thing to feel the pleasure of having a functional space (it's easier to find my things; I'm not tripping over toys; my toddler has better focus when the room isn't cluttered; I have space to work on my hobbies) and quite another to feel the satisfaction of having met a moral standard (I'm good enough; I'm a good mom today; I am meeting expectations; I'm a "real" adult). What you say to yourself when your house is clean fuels what you say to yourself when it's dirty. If you're good when it's clean, you must then be bad when it's not.

The good news is that you can simply choose to assign your chronic laundry pile a completely different meaning. Instead of thinking, "I can never keep up," instead say to yourself, "I am so grateful to have so many clothes." Upon your seeing a dirty kitchen, your inner voice may say something like, "I am such a hot mess," but challenge yourself to think of something else it could mean. "I cooked my family dinner three nights in a row" is a true statement. If care tasks are morally neutral, then having not showered or brushed your hair in three weeks does not mean "I am disgusting" but instead simply means "I am having a hard time right now."

Let me tell you what the mess in my home means. It means I'm alive. Dirty dishes mean I've fed myself. Scattered hobby supplies mean I am creative. Scattered toys and mess mean I am a fun mom. The stacked boxes in the hall mean I was thoughtful enough to order what we need. The clothes strewn on the floor mean I had a full day.

And occasionally mess means I'm struggling with depression or stress. But those aren't moral failings either—and neither is that moldy coffee cup I keep not taking to the kitchen.

Instead of . . . Try saying:

- **Chores → care tasks**
  Chores are obligations. Care tasks are kindness to self.

- Cleaning → resetting the space

  Cleaning is endless. Resetting the space has a goal.
- It's so messy in here! → this space has reached the end of its functional cycle

  It's so messy in here feels like failure. This space has reached the end of its functional cycle is morally neutral.
- Good enough is good enough → good enough is perfect

  Good enough is good enough sounds like settling for less. Good enough is perfect means having boundaries and reasonable expectations.

Shortcut: skip to chapter 7.

care tasks
are functional

I want you to stop caring for your home. You might think it's important to care for your home, but your home is an inanimate object—it's building materials and paint. It might need maintenance, but it doesn't deserve to be cared for. *You* are a person. You deserve to be cared for. I want your home to care for you. How do we do that? By focusing on function.

how to find the function

You can break down care tasks into three layers. At their foundation, care tasks have the basic function of keeping your body or space safe and healthy. This is represented by the bottom layer of the cupcake. The icing on the cake, so to say, is things that increase your comfort. The cherry on top is just things that make you happy. When we understand what really matters to us in terms of safety, comfort, and happiness, we can begin to let go of others' judgments of how our spaces must look. One person may be perfectly comfortable and happy in a space that is significantly messier and less organized than another person.

The health and safety aspects of care tasks are pretty universal, but the comfort and happiness layers are unique to each individual. For example, let's take the care task of changing your sheets. It's hygienic for everyone to remove dust, sweat, and dead skin cells from their bed. Many people would agree that it's more comfortable not to have little bits of stuff tracked into the bed from feet or pets. But only some people really identify that making their bed makes them happy. Lots of people could care less.[2]

It's easier to tolerate the repetitive nature of care tasks if we let go of moral messages and isolate the functional reason for doing them. The idea that "I'll just have to do this again tomorrow" can be exhausting and de-motivating. Yet most of us never think, "Why bother eating? I'm just going to be hungry again in a few hours." We understand that eating is functional. We need to give our bodies calories and nutrients so we can go about making a joyful life.

Try writing down your various care tasks and isolating the functional reason for doing each of them. Take the task of sweeping our floors. A moral view might say, "A dirty floor is disgusting. A floor should be clean. Real adults keep their floors clean."

---

2 See the appendix for more examples.

Notice all the value statements and the perfectionistic, all or nothing view. Also notice that in order to fulfill this value standard the floor must be *clean at all times*. Instead, **challenge yourself to find a functional reason to clean the floors**. For me, I do not like the feeling of little bits of stuff sticking to the bottom of my feet. That bothers me. When there are things cluttering the floor, I often trip. Those are two great functional reasons for me to pick up and sweep my floor. I still may not do this every day, or even often if I am really struggling. But with a functional rather than moral view, my brain may go, "Let's sweep a path from the bedroom to the kitchen because I deserve to walk that path without tripping or getting dirt on my feet." All of a sudden, the task isn't about measuring up but instead about caring for self.

Let's try this exercise with our kitchen counter. A moral message I may have is "a good wife keeps her kitchen clean." This will cause me to either stress out unless the whole kitchen is spotless or be so overwhelmed with the idea that I must clean the whole kitchen that I feel paralyzed and do nothing. Either way I am exhausted. When I ask myself what makes my kitchen function for me I can begin to identify concrete needs such as having enough clean dishes for the day, enough clear counter space to prepare food safely, access to my sink and a stove burner, and an empty trash can. Suddenly all that is really required fits on a short, finite list. I can do a few things to feel like I have cared for my needs. Then move on. If I have the time and energy to continue on and clean the whole kitchen, great! But if not, I can move on without guilt. Now my space is serving me and not the other way around.

what is quickest is not always what's functional

If I had a dollar for every time I have been told to "clean as you go" or "just don't put it down; put it away," I would solve my care task problems because I would be a bazillionaire and would hire people to do everything for me. Alas, those habits have never worked for me.

I understand why people offer this advice. It does make sense on paper that putting something away right after you use it or cleaning up a mess right after you make it is the quickest way to maintain a tidy home. But the quickest way to do something may not be the most functional way for every person. I once spent a whole day trying to clean as I go and by the end I was stressed, exhausted, and yelling at everyone. Oh, and my house wasn't even that clean.

Trying to clean up every mess as it's made fractures my attention span and makes me feel frazzled. The concentration it takes to keep track of every item I use and return it to its home immediately makes it difficult to enjoy the moment. To top it all off, my young children are fast as lightning and their needs are often immediate.

Cleaning up the breakfast mess may only take ten minutes, but in that time my oldest has taken her pajamas off on the kitchen floor, pulled out a box of LEGOs, and fallen and scraped her knee. Cleaning up breakfast, picking up floor pj's, tidying LEGOs, and getting a Band-Aid cannot physically happen all at once. Just as I get done kissing boo-boos and putting clothes on the oldest, the youngest has asked for more milk and shat her pants. The list of things that needs to be cleaned simply grows faster than any one person can move. Not to mention I *must* get these children out the door in the next five minutes or we won't have time to go to the park before nap time.

Even when I'm by myself, I tend to wander excitedly from project to project without quite wrapping up the former one before beginning the next. This isn't a flaw. I *like* spending my day this way. It's fun and enjoyable for me. It does make for a bigger mess at the end of the day, but the answer isn't to force myself into a clean-as-you-go habit that doesn't work for my brain. The solution is to develop achievable and even rewarding strategies for tackling a larger end of day reset. That's what works for me and it's just as valid as the choice of those who prefer to clean as they go.

At the end of the day I typically have a big pile of dirty dishes. I've been known to spend ten minutes organizing them on the countertop before loading them into the dishwasher. People almost always scratch their head and say, "You know the right way to do dishes would have been faster that what you just did." And they aren't wrong. It is, technically speaking, faster to load dishes directly from the sink into the dishwasher or, better yet, directly from using them into the dishwasher throughout the day. But sometimes the "right" way of doing something creates barriers for certain executive functioning skills. Sometimes the simple reason is that the right way is not enjoyable and so it gets procrastinated. **For a lot of people, finding a method that bypasses the most executive functioning barriers or that makes a task a little less intolerable is better than what's "quickest." In the end, the approach that you are motivated to do and enjoy doing is the most "efficient," because you are actually doing it and not avoiding it.**

gentle self-talk: find the compassionate observer

When you have functional barriers, things pile up fast. It's not uncommon to suddenly find yourself in an overwhelming mess. The more you stare at it, the more defeated you feel, the less motivation you have, the more you avoid it, and the more it piles up.

One reason that popular programs for cleaning don't work for everyone is that they so often fail to address what is happening emotionally around the task. When we find ourselves struggling with care tasks, we can usually identify two voices:

the inner bully

When we are stuck in this cycle, we often are suffering under the constant barrage of our inner bully. "Look at this filth; you are so lazy." "How could you let it get like this?" "You don't deserve a shower; look what you've done to your room."

the little self

In turn, our little self (the one being bullied) grieves. "Why is this so easy for other people?" "What's wrong with me?" "I'm failing."

This right here is an abusive relationship and someone needs to step in. That someone is you. Wait, you are bullying yourself and you are going to step in? Yes. There is a *third voice in there*. Think back to the last kind thing you did for another human or animal. Remember the compassion you felt? The gentleness with which you helped them? That person. This is your compassionate self. This self feels empathy for others because they are worthy of love, and this self wants to give it to them.

Do you remember the last time you observed beauty? Maybe it was the way your daughter's hair curled at the nape of her neck. Or the way your partner laughed. A sunset, a flower, a rainy day that made you feel peaceful. That person is in there too. That is your observant self. They see things from the outside with an eye for what is worthy. This person is your compassionate observer. And they are about to step in.

the compassionate observer

The next time the bully starts talking and the little self starts shrinking, you can call on your compassionate observer self. They say to the bully, "You are not being helpful and I need you to stop." And they turn to the little self and say, "I know you are in pain, and I know you feel like you are failing. But you aren't. It's not a moral failing to be untidy. Being unwell and struggling do not make you unworthy of kindness. You are going to be okay. I am here with you." Think of what you would say to a friend who was struggling and turn the message inward.

We know now that care tasks are morally neutral and have nothing to do with being a good or bad person. We also are learning that we deserve kindness regardless of our level of functioning. Now it's time to practice internalizing it by letting our compassionate observer rein in the inner bully and show kindness to the little self.

A literal explanation: All of the thoughts in your head come from you. Sometimes you have angry thoughts about yourself such as, "God, I'm so worthless!" and sometimes you have sad thoughts about yourself like, "I really wish someone could help me and I feel alone." This exercise is about purposefully preparing to respond to any angry thoughts—either in your mind or in a journal—with something that is kind, the way you would with a friend. If a friend said, "I am so worthless," you might say, "I think it's pretty normal to make mistakes. That doesn't mean you aren't worthy." When you think sad thoughts, you can respond the way you would comfort a friend: "I'm sorry you feel alone. It's okay to cry." Even though you know it's still you saying it to yourself and even if you don't believe it yet, the exercise begins to help you decrease the number of distressing thoughts you have over time.

The Compassionate Observer is a concept created by Kristin Neff, PhD. She has this and more exercises for cultivating self-compassion at https://self-compassion.org/.

Shortcut: skip to chapter 10.

how to keep house while drowning

organized is not the same as tidy

When we focus on function, organization becomes easier. Someone once asked me, "How did you get so organized?" To which I replied, "Once I realized I did not have to be tidy to be organized, the second half of my life began!"

Organization means having a place for everything in your home and having a system for getting it there. "Tidiness" and "messiness" describe how quickly things go back to their place. A tidy person typically returns things to their home immediately whereas a messy person does not.

Some people are messy because they are not organized. They don't have adequate storage solutions or they struggle to find permanent homes for their things. However, you can be messy and organized. In my home, almost everything has a place, but ADHD and two small kids mean things don't really get returned to their places very quickly. Instead, I have routines like closing duties and techniques like five things tidying that create space in my day to reset my space. Being organized means tidying moves more quickly and makes my life more functional and cleaning less overwhelming.

My countertops are almost never tidy, but they are functional. There is a difference between a countertop that is cluttered to the point that you can't use it to do the things you want to do and a countertop that is cluttered because you are actively and currently using it to do the things you want to do. A functional countertop is not morally superior to a nonfunctional countertop. The difference here isn't an external measurement of whether you are doing it right. The difference is your enjoyment of your own space. And you do deserve to enjoy your space.

organization does not have to be pretty

One reason why we have a hard time setting up systems that work for us is that we confuse an organized space with an aesthetically pleasing space. You can spend a lot of time organizing things the "Instagrammable" way only to find that the system is not functional for you, especially if keeping it pretty requires extra steps you don't always have the capacity to do. I once got the great idea from an organizational magazine to buy a clear shoe box for every pair of shoes I owned. "Then I can see them all and they will look so organized!" I told myself. Well, the truth is that the extra steps of putting shoes inside their own boxes and trying to pull the shoes I wanted from the bottom of the stack created more frustration than it was worth. I kept exactly one of those shoe boxes for my only pair of expensive heels and threw the rest of the shoes into a big basket all together.

I love a calming visual as much as the next person, but it's important to remember that not everything has to be aesthetically pleasing to be organized and not everything aesthetically pleasing is functional! No one is coming to take photographs of the vitamins, Pledge spray, salt, and cup of pens sitting on my island turntable. But that doesn't mean it's not organized. The truth is that if it's where you meant it to be, then it's organized.

In conclusion: being messy is not a moral failing, tidy is simply a preference, organization is functional, and you deserve to function. How would your approach to functional organization change if you threw pretty out the window?

An Ode to Baskets

Big baskets, little baskets, clear baskets, wicker baskets,
*   baskets from the Dollar Tree, baskets that I got*
*   for free.*
Baskets of shoes, baskets of books, baskets in all my
*   crannies and nooks.*
And here's the key, here's the trick:
the baskets go where the stuff already went.
Laundry that ends up on the dining room floor,

put a basket there and there's mess no more.
The stress of a cluttered counter easily ends
when you put it all in a box or a bin.
If you're feeling fancy you could purchase a
        basket's cousin
such as a tray or a lazy Susan.
My organizational system is, on its face,
just putting a basket in the right place.

susie with depression

We know that two people can go through the same thing and be affected by it very differently. The same disorder or barrier does not present the same way in everyone. For every person with cancer making Marvel movies, there is someone at home who can't do anything but survive the day and attempt to eat. It's rarely about who is trying harder or who is a better person but instead about individual capacity. Individual capacity is shaped by biology, psychology, and environment. Just because Susie with six kids and depression can keep an immaculate house does not mean you are morally inferior if you cannot. If Susie worked hard for that house and it made her happy she gets to be proud of it. And if you worked hard to eat a meal today, you get to feel proud of that too without any guilt about the state of your home. If you cannot do it like Susie, your only two options are to try to be like Susie and be miserable and burnt-out or to try to do things within your capacity and be whole and happy. Neither of these choices affects Susie's life in the slightest.

And remember, while you compare yourself to others, convinced that if you could be like them you'd be happy and worthy, there is probably someone comparing themselves to you, thinking the same. We are all somebody's Susie.

gentle skill building: kick-starting motivation

I bought an exercise bike.

"Okay, but will you really use it?" Michael said with a kind but knowing tone.

After I gave him what can only be described as an award-winning presentation on the benefits of exercise (boosting serotonin and dopamine helps with mood regulation and focus) and told him that having such a convenient way to exercise at home would ensure that, for the first time in my life, I would actually stick with exercising for more than a week, he reluctantly agreed it sounded like a good idea.

I started out strong, riding multiple times a week for a month and getting up to forty-five-minute rides. This time was going to be different!

Sound familiar? You probably know where this is going. I have used the exercise bike exactly once in the past two months. The fact that Michael has come to love it and ride it regularly is probably the only reason he hasn't gotten mad at me for getting it.

When my kids went back to preschool in the fall I told myself I would just start by riding for five minutes after I dropped them off. That would get the ball rolling.

The first day of school came and I didn't do the five minutes.

In the past, when I predictably fall off after the first wave of motivation the guilt sets in. "You've done it again, KC. Just like the last thing. Stop kidding yourself." Followed by a few attempts to get back on track, which also fail. I never manage to recapture that initial motivation and in turn give up completely and feel guilty whenever I look at the thing.

The great dream of getting into the exercise groove followed by dismal compliance is probably not a new story for anyone reading right now (and if it wasn't an exercise habit that couldn't stick, it's journaling or meditating or keeping your room clean). That part of this story was unfortunately not that different. But here is what has been different.

Instead of concluding the problem was that I just needed to try harder the next day, I said out loud, "I didn't get on the bike yesterday for five minutes even though I do want to get on the bike. This tells me that five minutes was too big of a goal. I wonder if I could get on for three minutes?"

I got on the bike planning to ride for three minutes. Then rode two minutes after that. The next day I got on for five minutes and did five more while I was it. Then we all got the stomach bug and I didn't ride for a week. But now I know I can do three minutes. I've found my on-ramp.[3]

---

3   The metaphor of an on-ramp is used to explain how you can make starting a task feel easier, in the same way that the entrance lane to a highway allows you to gradually merge onto the road.

Maybe I'll get back into a rhythm of doing it more often and maybe it will keep being inconsistent. **One thing I know is that if I keep the shame removed I can keep the on-ramp open.** The worst-case scenario here is I sometimes get three minutes of health and mood benefits.

the problem of task initiation

One of the most common concerns I hear from those struggling with care tasks is, "I want to get things done, but I just can't motivate myself to do it."

Now, problems with motivation are valid, but I want you to consider if it's really motivation you are lacking. Motivation means a desire or drive to do something and a recognition that you see that thing as worth doing. If you don't understand why doing laundry matters or you feel so awful that you just think you don't deserve clean clothes so what's the point, you are struggling to find motivation. If, however, you want clean clothes, you feel your life would be better with clean clothes, and you would like to be able to do the laundry you've been staring at for hours but just can't seem to make yourself do, that's not a lack of motivation. That is a problem with task initiation.

If you have a diagnosis like ADHD, autism, PTSD, or depression (and many others), you are probably familiar with task initiation problems, because those diagnoses famously create problems with executive functioning, of which task initiation is one. If you've been living with situational factors that affect executive functioning like trauma, grief, chronic stress, or sleep deprivation, you may also be experiencing issues with task initiation.

Take a deep breath here. You are not lazy. You just need help circumventing some barriers.

Task initiation barriers usually present themselves as difficulties in transitions. So I'm sitting in a chair and I need to go do dishes, but it's very difficult to initiate the transition from sitting comfortably in my chair to getting up to do dishes. What I need to do here is find a way to create momentum. Just like with my exercise bike, we can widen the entry point to the task by creating an on-ramp.

Ideas that help with task initiation:

creating movement momentum with music

One way to widen the entry point is to use music. Moving from sitting down to up and dancing is a big transition. But moving from sitting down to wiggling your toes to the beat is a small one. From there the transition to moving your legs and arms to the song is also a small step. It's another small step to move your whole body in a fantastic chair dance. Now you're already moving, so you might as well stand  up! When you're up and active, it's only a small transition to moving towards the sink. Oftentimes momentum will pick up from there.

We know that "neurons that fire together wire together" and that your brain can associate feelings with experiences. If you dance every day to the same happy song with your baby, or your pet, or a friend on FaceTime and after a week play that song while folding laundry or doing dishes, your brain will associate happiness with that song and will provide a little pleasure reward.

permission to start

"I'm going to make myself do the dishes now." "I forced myself to shower today." Let's try a perspective shift. Instead of bullying yourself into finishing a task, instead try giving yourself permission to start a task. Let yourself get a little done. Say, "I am going to do one dish." Often you'll find that motivation kicks in after you have already started. It's stressful to try to summon up 100 percent of the momentum to do something while sitting on the couch. Let yourself use 5 percent energy to do 5 percent of the task. Maybe you keep going. Maybe you don't. That's okay. Anything worth doing is worth doing partially.

moving towards

Instead of "I need to finish this" or even "I need to start this," begin to say to yourself, "How can I move towards this task?" When you want to get your kitchen reset before you sit down for the evening, moving towards can just mean going and standing in the kitchen. Do nothing; do anything; sit by the sink; look at your phone while you lean on the counter. Even this placeholder step can help create enough momentum to eventually pick up one dish.

built-in wait times

What activities in your life do you enjoy that have built-in wait times? Maybe it's waiting for the kettle to boil or for cookies to bake. Next time you want to do a care task, start an enjoyable task and use the wait time to start a care task. Knowing that there is a finish line can lower the barrier to entry. My favorite trick is to cut myself a break on cooking dinner and order DoorDash, using the wait time to get some things done. Knowing I can be totally finished when the food arrives feels motivating to me.

bundling

If you tend to avoid care tasks because they are boring, choose something you can enjoy during the task: a Netflix show, a podcast, an audiobook, et cetera. Don't just limit yourself to home care tasks either. A good podcast or audiobook while you shower can make all the difference.

body doubling

Have you ever noticed it's easier to do something when a friend is with you? Even if they don't help, there is something about the presence of another person that can make doing tasks easier. Ask a friend to spend time with you while you do care tasks. You can even call them on the phone.

timed cleaning

One of my favorite tools is the visual timer. It helps in so many ways! Sometimes when we think of a task that seems unpleasant, like unloading the dishwasher, our brain tells us that the task is going to take much longer than it actually does. Other times tasks like cleaning our bedroom feel so huge it's overwhelming to even start. In those instances it's helpful to set a timer for a small increment of time that you feel you can stomach. Usually between five and fifteen minutes. The visual color helps your brain conceptualize the amount of time left more clearly than a regular clock or timer. When using a timer, you realize that unloading the dishwasher only takes four minutes! When you are cleaning your bedroom, the timer gives you permission to stop after fifteen minutes regardless of whether the task is done. Feel like you're in the groove now and want to keep going? Great! Want to stop? That's allowed too.

(Note: The visual timer is also helpful for those who experience time blindness. When you have forty-five minutes to get ready for work, setting a visual timer makes time management easier because you can see the time remaining as a percentage of time rather than a number. This is also the reason it's great for kids!)

There are a few brands that sell visual timers. Time Timer and Secura are two good brands. If audible ticking bothers you, make sure to get one where you can turn that feature off.

care tasks are cyclical

W hen I became a stay-at-home mom, I signed up to make sure my family always had clean clothes, not that they never had dirty ones.

This is your gentle reminder that mounds of dirty laundry are not a failure. It doesn't matter if you're "never caught up on laundry." It only matters if everyone has clean clothes to wear when they need them. If your laundry system produces clean clothes, then it's working. If you'd like to make it more efficient, then get creative! But remember that upgrading your laundry system can only increase your functioning, not your worth.

you do not have to line up every care cycle

This was a comment I received on one of my videos on TikTok where I was talking

I mean it's not a hoarder's house but it definitely isn't clean either...

about cleaning my house. It's always funny to me how "clean house" and "dirty house" are presented as these absolute states with no gray area in between.

You are not morally obligated to make every single care cycle line up at the "just done" state and hold it there always. As I write this my kitchen island is messy and my living room floors are immaculate. My laundry hasn't been put away for three days and my playroom is dust-free. Eventually I will get around to cleaning the island, and by then there will be dust in the playroom and dirt on the floors. My kids will come home from school today and get busy destroying the playroom while I put up the laundry. **Not everything has to be clean at the same time.**

I could exhaust myself making it look like a showroom all the time, but then I wouldn't have time to take my kids to go get Halloween costumes today, or talk to a friend on the phone for an hour, or write this book.

why clean when it will look like this tomorrow?

A really common defeating message that we say to ourselves is "What's the point of picking up? It's just going to look like this again tomorrow." I find this stems from that binary view of care tasks that they can be only either done or not done and that done is the superior state. But keeping everything done isn't the point. Keeping things functional is the point because here's the thing: it will look like that again tomorrow *only* if I clean it today. If I don't clean it, it will be even more messy because we live here and we create mess. And if tomorrow's mess on top of today's mess is going to make my space not function for me, then it's time to reset the space.

I tidy things up not because it's bad that it's messy but because it has reached the end of that cycle of functionality and I need to reset it so it can have another twenty-four hours of it serving me.

Shortcut: skip to chapter 13.

how to keep house while drowning

gentle skill building: setting functional priorities

egardless of how tightly we embrace the functional view of care tasks, the reality is there are seasons of life when there are more care tasks to do than there is time in the day (or energy in the body). Work, relationships, activism, care tasks, hobbies, and, for some, parenting all compete for that same time and energy.[4] Even if we understand that doing everything perfectly is impossible, most of us still have a hard time shaking the constant guilt about how things *should* look. It can be a struggle deciding exactly what to prioritize when time and energy are short.

One tool that can be very helpful when deciding how to prioritize and de-prioritize items is the 9 square. Pick an area of your life. School, activism, parenting, et cetera. For our example, we will use self-care. Write a list of things you think are important for your self-care. First, think of the self-care items that have the high-

---

4   Christine Miserandino is a disability advocate who articulates this in her concept of Spoon Theory, which is a helpful resource in understanding chronic illness.

est impact on your mental health. Let's say taking your medication, showering, and having clean dishes.

Next list those item that have a medium impact (rest, socializing, and exercise) and those that have a lower impact (laying out tomorrow's outfit, folding clothes, and cleaning your floors). You can choose as many items as you'd like. Next, divide them into those things that take low effort, medium effort, or a high amount of effort. Place your items in the corresponding squares in the chart.

Once the chart is filled out, you can use it to determine what to focus on. When things in your life are ideal, you may strive to do all of the squares. Come under some stress and the black square is de-prioritized without guilt. Come under a bit more stress or for a prolonged period and the dark blue squares are de-prioritized in order to focus on the light blue squares.

It may seem odd that laying out an outfit for tomorrow is prioritized over exercise. **But this way of thinking of priorities allows you to do the most good with the least amount of energy.**

This tool isn't meant to tell you what to do as much as give you permission to not feel guilty about what you don't do. If you find it helpful, a good friend or a therapist can help you fill it out and act as validation when deciding what priority level you are on. It's helpful when seeing your dirty floor to replace "I just can't keep up" with "I've de-prioritized floors for a more important task right now."

Take this parenting example. When I've got a lot going on, I don't fret whether our food is organic, since that is level 3 priority. During especially difficult times (like, say, being quarantined with two small children for months on end) I de-prioritize limiting screen time, getting daily outside play, and keeping toys nonelectronic. I'm not saying they aren't important, just acknowledging that if I only have limited capacity, not yelling, helping my kids understand their feelings, physical affection, reading, and telling my kids I'm proud of them are going to have a greater impact on them than the other items (and,

more importantly, a greater impact than attempting to do it all and, as a result, not being able to do any of it).

women and care tasks

In our society, care tasks have historically been left to women. Unfortunately, as the role of the daughter, wife, and mother has widened to allow for personal ambitions, careers, and equal partnership in the working world, the pattern of placing the main responsibility for a family's care tasks on the women in the family still remains. This leads many women to be overloaded with never-ending work from both their "real" jobs and relationships and their invisible duties of care tasks. **Although men may struggle with completing care tasks, they are less likely to receive the message from society that they are not worthy of love or not valid as a human if they are not good at these tasks.** This distress becomes heavy and can permeate the mental health of women. But it does not have to be this way. Regardless of your gender, reflect on what messages you received about women and care tasks. How have these messages affected your view of women and your relationships with them? How has it impacted your feelings about your own gender?

gentle skill building: laundry

it's not failure. it's laundry

My Postpartum Laundry Routine

1. Put a laundry basket in every room in the house

2. Put laundry into washer

3. Come back in eight hours when it smells like mildew because I forgot about it

4. Wash again

5. Put laundry into dryer

6. Come back in twenty-four hours when it's all wrinkled

7. Unload clothes from dryer onto laundry room floor

8. Leave it there for seven to ten business days

9. Look at myself in the mirror and remind myself being bad at laundry is not a moral failing and I'm doing just fine.

I did not fold even one article of clothing until my baby was seven months old. For seven months my entire family lived out of a giant pile of clean clothes that spanned the entire surface of my laundry room floor. I could occasionally get it into the washer and transferred to the dryer in between toddler tantrums and baby screams, but I just could never get any further. One day, as if by magic, I ended up with a little time to go fold some laundry. If I had spent those seven months telling myself I was a piece of shit every time I looked at that laundry pile, I probably would not have had the motivation to do it despite having the time. That is because if a laundry pile represents failure and I'm already struggling with a newborn and a pandemic and an energetic toddler, my brain, which is trying desperately to avoid pain and seek pleasure (or at least relief from pain), is never going to give me the green light to lean in to yet another painful experience like spending thirty minutes in my failure pile of laundry. But it's not failure. It's laundry. Keeping it morally neutral actually helped me get it done.

hacking my laundry: out of moral neutrality comes permission

This self-compassionate approach carried me through several months of living in survival mode. It also laid the foundation for the life-changing revelation about function I had one day while engaging in a rare moment of folding clothes. I looked down at the baby onesie I was folding and asked myself a shocking question.

"Why am I folding baby onesies?"

I had no answer. They didn't really wrinkle and even if they did it's not like anyone cares if a baby is wearing a wrinkled onesie. I'd probably change it four times before lunch anyways.

"These . . . don't . . . need to be folded."

I said it out loud, bracing myself for . . . the laundry police? I'm not sure. There were rules to laundry, but for the first time I stopped asking myself how laundry should be done and started questioning in what way laundry could be functional for me.

I looked around the piles I was sitting in. Fleece pajamas, sweat pants, underwear, gym shorts.

"Almost none of this . . . almost none of this needs to be folded."

I whispered it to myself, as if the laundry gods would smite me at that very moment.

I went through the pile, picking out the few items that truly needed to remain wrinkle-free for work or just out of preference. It took me one minute to hang these. The rest I put away unfolded in under three.

Oh my god. What other rules am I following that don't make sense?

rethinking laundry rules

1. ~~Laundry baskets go in bedrooms~~ Laundry baskets go everywhere. They go in every room even and especially in the kitchen and living room.

2. ~~Wash clothes when the bins are full~~ Wash only on Mondays and wash everything on Monday. Eventually this day will become synonymous with laundry and it will be easier to remember.

3. ~~Sort darks and whites~~ Load everything together. Do not sort. Wash on cold.

4. ~~Transfer from washer to dryer quickly~~ Set a timer once the washer starts. Set timer again once dryer starts.

5. ~~Fold clothes~~ Create multiple bins/baskets for clothes and toss them in unfolded. Hang a few shirts.

how to keep house while drowning

6. ~~Put away in everyone's different closets in their room~~ All clothes are stored in one room, which is the en suite closet off the laundry area. It makes no sense to take clothes to three different closets when I am the person dressing all three of those people. Sit on butt and put away every family member's laundry in under eight minutes without moving.

making laundry serve you

Laundry does not have to be done the way you have always been taught to do it. Here are some other questions you can ask yourself to find what works for you.

- What preconceived ideas do you have about laundry? When we get rid of thinking there is a morally right or valid adult way of doing laundry, we see the possibilities of making laundry functional for ourselves.

- Does all laundry really need to be folded? Undies, baby clothes, athletic shorts, and pajamas usually do just fine being bunched up in a drawer or a clean laundry basket. Perhaps it's a more manageable task to pick out the few things you would like to be wrinkle-free and hang them up, leaving the rest to sit happily in a basket or drawer where you can access them.

- Does laundry have to be put away? Who says? If folding it and leaving it in the laundry room or a clean basket works for you, there is no reason to go through the extra steps of putting it in drawers.

- Does laundry have to be done in huge loads, or am I better served by washing a small load every day of the essentials?

- Does sorting my laundry before I wash and dry it make it more likely to get done or a more enjoyable task for me?

- Would you like to have fewer clothes so there is less to wash? Would you like to start buying wrinkle-free fabrics so you don't have to worry about leaving clothes in the dryer?

- If you can afford it, would you like to just outsource this task completely and move on with your awesome life? Consider hiring someone to come weekly or bi-weekly and do laundry. Consider if you would rather take everything to the wash and fold service at the laundromat.[5]

when you need a laundry reset

You can read about all the creative laundry systems in the world and it won't be helpful if you feel so paralyzed by your current mountains of laundry that you feel you can never get to a place where you can even implement a new system. It's always valid to send everything out to a wash and fold and just get it over with. If that's in the budget and that blank slate would be helpful to you, let it rip.

People talk a lot about the benefit of downsizing your wardrobe, but since that in and of itself is a huge undertaking, it's not really a great starting point when you feel like you're drowning. **However, we can fake a closet downsize and still get all of the benefits without having to deal with the intense decision-making process real downsizing requires.** Pick out a week's worth of clothing to launder and pack everything else away in bags or Rubbermaid bins until a time when you can deal with it. Pick a day to launder your clothes, and if you feel up to it add back in a few items at a time. It may feel better to have more space

---

5   See appendixes for more ideas on laundry systems.

without the clothes everywhere and be more manageable to keep up with your new smaller wardrobe.

not quite dirty but not quite clean

People always ask me what to do with those clothes that are not quite dirty enough to go into the dirty clothes hamper, but because you've worn them they're a little dirty and you might wear them again. In my experience, clothes like this often end up on a chair somewhere. I like to start by saying that if the clothes chair is working for you there is no reason to change that. We're just talking about what functions and if you have a space to house those "not quite dirty, not quite clean" clothes—be it a chair or a basket—and it doesn't bother you, then there's really no problem.

If I have a shirt that I wore that day and it's not quite dirty enough to go into the dirty clothes hamper, I just . . . put it back with the clean clothes. It's fine. It's amazing, actually. Clothes in my house existing in either a laundry basket or in the closet simplifies my life.

Remember, at the end of the day it's really not that important whether you figure out a way to "stay on top of your laundry." What's important is learning to treat yourself with compassion and have a kind inner dialogue about laundry. If you never figure it out but have less shame in your life and more joy, I'd say that's a win.

you can't save the rain forest if you're depressed

You are not responsible for saving the world if you are struggling to save yourself. If you must use paper plates for meals or throw away recycling in order to gain better functioning, you should do so. When you are functioning again, you will gain the capacity to do real good for the world. In the meantime, your job is to survive.

Realistically, when you are struggling to function you are not choosing between recycling and not recycling; you are choosing between letting the cardboard pile up and staying paralyzed and throwing the cardboard out and being able to get unstuck enough to move forward. Either way the recycling isn't getting done that day. However, if you sacrifice a few weeks of cardboard (or Tupperware, or paper, or plastics), you may well have a chance at gaining a functioning human being capable of engaging in and making a difference in important causes like environmentalism.

Feeling shame for not being sustainable, for eating meat, or for purchasing fast fashion when you are fighting to get through the day is not going to cause you to magically gain the ability to do something different. Shame is a horrible long-term motivator. It is more likely to contribute to dysfunction and continued cycles of unsustainable practices.

nobody is doing all the good things all the time

When I think of all the good things I could be doing—whether it's environmentalism, activism, or other altruistic acts—I try to categorize them into two tiers. The first tier lists the standards I expect myself to be accountable to at all times and in all areas of my life. This is also the tier I welcome anyone to hold me accountable for. For me, this tier includes ensuring my behavior is not racist, sexist, classist, homophobic, transphobic, or ableist, that I always refrain from abusing or exploiting others, and that I always act with honesty and integrity.

The second tier includes morally good things that aren't absolutes but that I participate in when possible: supporting small businesses, donating money, volunteering my time, recycling, avoiding fast fashion, reducing waste, prioritizing businesses with ethical practices. I am only accountable to myself and my inner circle for how I organize this tier.

No person can do all the good things all the time and expecting yourself to just sets up an oppressive perfectionism to which no one can live up. Imperfection is required for a good life.

drop the plastic balls

J ennifer Lynn Barnes, a YA author, tweeted:

One time, I was at a Q&A with Nora Roberts, and someone asked her how to balance writing and kids, and she said that the key to juggling is to know that some of the balls you have in the air are made of plastic & some are made of glass.

When you are struggling to function, it's important to identify what are your glass balls. Feeding yourself, caring for your children and/or animals, taking your medication, and addressing your mental health are all examples of glass balls. Dropping them would have devastating consequences and likely cause you to drop all the balls. Recycling, veganism, and shopping local are plastic balls. They may be important, but they will not shatter your life if you drop them in the way the glass balls will. Plastic balls will fall to the floor and stay intact so you can pick them up again later. Glass balls will not.

Literal explanation: If you cannot do everything you want to do, it's important to identify which care tasks are necessary for you to function and prioritize them until you are in a place where you can do more. For example, if you are in a very stressful time in your life and cannot stay on top of cleaning your cat's litter box and sorting the recycling, it is best to stop sorting the recycling and use your energy to find a routine that works for getting your cat's litter box scooped frequently. Not recycling for a time will have an extremely small impact on the world, but not caring for your cat will have a huge impact on your cat.

my pre-pasted toothbrushes

My personal executive functioning kryptonite is brushing my teeth. When I was going to school or working, it was never a problem. The daily ritual of standing at the vanity every morning and getting ready to leave the house coupled with the motivation that I didn't want anyone to be grossed out by my breath made it easy. When I had my first daughter, I struggled mightily to get my teeth brushed. Not only was I not really going anywhere, but the "wake up and get ready" morning ritual had been replaced by "get woken up by a screaming baby and run as fast as you can to feed said baby." Sleep deprivation, being homebound, and focusing on the new and overwhelming experience of caring for a newborn left brushing my teeth as a rogue task with no home in my daily rhythm.

When my second daughter was born amid the lockdown of the pandemic, the old problem of brushing my teeth returned full force. Add postpartum depression and undiagnosed ADHD to the list and it wasn't long before it became The Impossible Task. After eighteen months of self-compassion and various adaptive routines that didn't seem to stick, I finally had an honest moment with myself and ordered a box of 144 prepasted toothbrushes. I kept them in a bowl by the front door and would grab one whenever I went by them to the kitchen or out the back door. I kept the used brushes in a mason jar until I could figure out a way to recycle them, but even I felt shame at all the single-use plastic.

"You know, those single-use masks everyone is wearing in the pandemic are made of plastic too," my friend Imani Barbarin said to me. Imani is a talented disability advocate who often speaks about the intersection of disability and environmentalism. She pointed out that the acceptable use of plastic is always set according to what a healthy person needs to be healthy (think masks, gloves, plastic prescription bottles, kinesiology tape . . . even home delivery supplements that individually package your daily vitamins), but when it comes to someone with a disability using plastic, everyone wants to shame them for killing the planet. "You need what you need," she said to me in a gentle but firm voice. She was right. Besides, if I didn't figure out how to brush my teeth more often, the impending dental visit was sure to require ten times the amount of plastic to fix the damage.

The truth is that it's not waste if you are using something to function. Running your sprinklers every day for fifteen minutes is wasting water because that's more water than your yard needs to live. Grocery stores and restaurants throw out good food daily and that's wasting food. Not getting a dripping faucet fixed when you can afford to is wasting water. But using something is not the same as wasting something. It's okay to use a paper plate to eat if you're depressed and otherwise would've struggled to eat at all. Someone with diabetes can use disposable needles and you can buy a fucking prepackaged salad so you eat. The impact that you could have on the world when you are fully functioning far outweighs the negligible negative impact that one household's disposable plastic or extra water usage will have. There may be times when your local officials ask you to curb resource use because of an imminent scarcity, and when that happens you can do your best to muddle through. But it's not wrong to prioritize your functioning and find other ways you can contribute to environmentalism.

Climate change is real. Environmentalism is important. But we are not going to fix the earth by shaming people with mental health and neurodiverse needs out of adaptive routines they need to function. Take that energy to Congress. Those who feel anger at someone with clinical depression or ADHD for not engaging in eco-optimal behaviors are seriously deluded.

One of the major tenets of health professions is harm reduction. No one is made functional overnight, and some people may always have barriers. The goal then is to take steps that reduce harm, first to self, then to those individuals around us, then to our community. You cannot jump right to community harm reduction before first addressing individual harm reduction. Therefore, if a newly widowed woman struggles to eat, she is released from the obligation of having an eco-perfect diet not because eating ethically is unimportant, but because when the real-world choices for someone are eating dairy or eating nothing, it is always the ethical choice to eat. It is always the ethical choice to encourage that person to eat whatever they can manage. Harm reduction is always ethical.

gentle skill building:
doing the dishes

I am going to talk about dishes now. Here are the ground rules:

- If you have cried over dishes in the past seven days—go buy paper plates.
- If your dishes have been in the sink for months—throw them away.
- If you are wanting to tackle the pile of dishes—read on.

step one: preparation

Eat something sweet. Get that blood sugar up and find a great song to put on. Get yourself a cute apron and a pair of dishwashing gloves.

step two: organization

Take your dishes out of the sink and stack them into categories: big utensils, little utensils, bowls, plates, cups, big bulky dishes, pots and pans, et cetera. Getting them organized helps because:

- You can often see there are not as many dishes as you thought.

- The act of organizing is usually rewarding to most brains. This subtle step helps keep motivation going.

- This usually takes five minutes and it clears your sink. If you get through those five minutes and decide you're done then although you still have dirty dishes, you now have a clean sink, and a clean sink is functional. It would be perfectly acceptable to wash straight out of the sink without sorting first, and you can still give yourself permission to stop after five minutes. However, then you still have dirty dishes and no clear sink. So I find the sorting to be a more functional approach.

step three: wash or load

Hand washers can then wash by category, giving themselves permission to stop after each category. Dishwasher owners load up their dishwasher by category. If you have a dishwasher, remember there is no rule saying you must unload it all at once. It's perfectly fine to unload a category at a time when you feel you can manage it.

hacking my dishes: the dirty-dish rack

I've made small functional upgrades in my dish routine, one at a time. I decided that the first step would be to move from leaving dishes out all over the house to taking them to the sink. It was quick, which was important when I was postpartum with a new-born and a two-year-old bouncing off the walls, and it ensured that dishes weren't left around the house too long to collect mold or bacteria.

I enjoyed this functional upgrade for months. Then I went on medication for postpartum depression and got more capacity. From there I decided to start loading those sink dishes into the dishwasher every night at 7:00 pm and run it. Some days I man-aged to unload it first; others I simply shoved the dirty dishes in with the clean ones and ran it all again. Sometimes even that was a stretch and on those days I aimed for simply putting the milk cups my kids needed in the dishwasher.

One day while perusing IKEA I saw a dish rack and was hit

with a moment of functional genius. The barrier to doing dishes was the feeling of being overwhelmed when I looked at the pile. If I were to place the dirty dishes into the dish rack as I used them, my sink would be empty and accessible and the dirty dishes would be organized, which greatly cut down on the feeling of being overwhelmed when it came time to load them up into the dishwasher. I even bought myself a second silverware basket to sit on the counter so I could fill it up all day and swap it with the clean basket from the washer at night. Now I have my very own little dirty-dish station. It's unconventional, but it works for me!

when you don't have kids

Can I tell you a something about having kids? While it did create more mess than I had before and it does make completing tasks more difficult at times, in some ways having kids actually made care tasks easier for me. Caring for kids naturally necessitates having a schedule. They wake up at a certain time, eat at a certain time, nap at a certain time, and go to bed at a certain time. I genuinely don't know how I would motivate myself to do closing duties every night if I didn't already have the forced routine of putting kids to bed at 7:00 pm. That's really the reason I find myself on my feet every night at the same time and why it's easy for me to roll right into closing duties.

My point is that having kids doesn't make care tasks easier or harder; it just makes them different. I was messy far before I ever had kids. I struggled to get dishes done as a single and childless person for my whole life. **You do not need to have children for your struggles with care tasks to be valid.** You are welcome here.

when it's hard to shower

It is more common than you would think for people to have barriers to hygiene. Whether those barriers are physical or mental, it is the care area where people feel the most shame in not being able to keep up. Remember that showering is functional and not moral. Millions of human beings existed before the invention of showers, and they managed to live and thrive without them. As with any care task, self-compassion is key. Shame is the enemy of functioning.

hygiene kit

The point of having a body is to carry yourself from joyful experience to joyful experience. We have functional reasons to clean that body because we want it to stay healthy and because it feels good. So if you have a physical or emotional barrier that makes taking a full shower so draining that you can't do anything else with your day, then it's perfectly fine to schedule a full shower once or twice a week depending on your capacity. For the rest of your time, you can use a hygiene kit. Placing multiple kits in areas of your home where you know you can access them easily can be helpful. For instance, I recommend that new mothers place these near a nursing station and that those with depression keep one at their bedside.

Hygiene Kit:

- Baby wipes
- Dry shampoo or oil
- Hairbrush
- Toothbrush and toothpaste (or disposable wisps)
- Mouthwash
- Face lotion
- Deodorant
- Essential oil or misting spray that smells good
- Washcloth

how to keep house while drowning

matted hair

If you have not washed your hair in a long time, it can be very painful emotionally to deal with matted hair. This is particularly true if you are already feeling depressed and have trouble getting out of bed. Remember to be kind to yourself. Touch your hair and body gently and remember that people who are having a hard time deserve compassion. You are people too.

I have fine, curly, Caucasian hair that begins to mat after several days in a bun with no brushing. Here's how I handle this:

1. I get into the shower, wet my hair, and apply a deep conditioner (I like Blueberry Bliss reparative leave-in conditioner). I do not shampoo first because greasy hair is easier to detangle.

2. I use huge fistfuls and then leave it to sit under a shower cap for twenty minutes.

3. After I remove the cap, I use a wide-tooth comb to divide into sections and start detangling from the bottom of my hair, holding at the root so it doesn't pull. After detangling I wash with shampoo and regular conditioner.

If you have spent many days or weeks in bed and the level of matting is very severe, the internet swears that miracle leave-in spray from It's a 10 is, as its name states, a miracle worker. Applying this spray to your hair, divide your hair into sections and use your fingers to detangle what you can starting from the bottom of the hair and working your way to the scalp. Once you've done what you can with your fingers, use a wide-tooth comb or a pick and repeat the process.

If you feel it may be a long time before you wash again, consider using a protective hair-style such as French braids. Silk scrunchies are better for buns, as they do not cause the hair to break like regular hair ties. A silk cap or pillowcase will help prevent matting and breakage.

The best method for detangling matted hair will depend on your hair type. I spoke with Dr. Raquel Martin to get some insight on the type of care that's best for Black hair when you're struggling. I'll let her take it from here.

Hi all. Dr. Martin here. I am going to share my insights into managing Black hair. When determining the best care routine for your hair, there are different things that you need to take into consideration including curl types, porosity level, and processing level. While my examples may not be exhaustive, I hope there is something in here that can help you. I have natural hair with a tight curl pattern that repels moisture, so it can quickly become difficult to manage. During times of significant transition, grief, and emotional distress, I could not even imagine lifting my arms long enough to do my hair.

When detangling Black hair, always start from the bottom, use a wide-tooth comb or Denman brush and detangle your hair while wet and with a leave-in conditioner. One of the best things that you can do to care for your hair when you don't feel like caring for yourself is wear a silk bonnet when you go to sleep or sleep on a silk pillowcase. Cotton pillowcases will take the moisture out of your hair and make it more difficult to manage. Remember that Black hair gets drier over time, and it's not necessary to place heavy oils on your actual hair; it is your scalp that requires the most oiling. You can use an essential oil, such as tea tree oil, mixed with a carrier oil, such as olive oil. Do not put pure essential oils on your hair; always mix it with a carrier oil. Tea tree oil is a great pick because it helps with itchiness and dryness and stimulates hair growth.

If you have chemically relaxed hair, your scalp may become more sensitive due to the new growth and be more difficult to manage than your processed ends. The hair closest to your roots will also likely revert to your natural texture, which could be curlier. Therefore, you may just want to do a twist out or braid out instead of having to go to a salon or manage it daily. These styles will make the disparity between your roots and ends less noticeable.

Protective styles give your hair a break and reduce the amount of manipulation required. These can include styles such as braids, faux locs, and twists. Try to not keep these hairstyles in longer than eight weeks because of increased buildup and scalp sensitivity over time. Headscarves can also be an easy solution to times when you do not feel like doing your hair. Putting one on does not take more than five minutes, they do not have to be fancy, and they look very nice.

Hello, this is KC again. It's useful for everyone to note that most salons will also de-mat your hair for an hourly fee. I find that being open about your struggles and stating that you are looking for someone who will help you without judgment is typically met with kindness.

brushing your teeth

It is not uncommon for brushing one's teeth to be the near-impossible task. This does not make you dirty or gross. It just makes you a person having a hard time. And people having a hard time deserve compassion. Here are some ideas for caring for your teeth when brushing is hard:

- Disposable wisps, flossers, and pre-pasted toothbrushes are all available and can be put into your bag, on your bedside, and in your car. Sometimes it's the getting to the bathroom that is the difficult part.

- Children's toothpaste has a sweeter flavor than adult toothpaste. Some find that moving away from the harsh mint flavors of adult toothpaste makes it easier to brush their teeth.

- Electric toothbrushes often do more cleaning in less time. Some even have timers and send reminders to your phone.

- Swishing your mouth with some Listerine can kill some bacteria in your mouth when you cannot get any brushing done. Remember that anything worth doing is worth doing half-assed.

- If you need to go to the dentist and are embarrassed that you have not maintained your dental care, ask to have an office visit with the dental hygienist first. Explain your anxiety and embarrassment. Explain your fear that if the doctor shames you, you may not come back. You may even ask that they note in your chart that you do not respond well to lecturing. Most medical providers truly do want you to continue getting medical care and will take the opportunity to be sensitive if you ensure they are informed of your needs.

Shortcut: skip to chapter 23.

caring for your body when you hate it

When I was seven, my mom took me to the SPCA and told me I could pick out a cat. I walked straight to the back of the rows of cages and found the rattiest little cat you've ever seen in your life. Her tail had been severed after she was hit by a car and her butt was oozing from fresh wounds and ointments. Without even looking at the other cats I announced to my mother that I wanted that one. I took her home and I cared for that cat. I got to know her and she became my friend, not because she appeared worthy but simply because I decided to care for her. My point is, sometimes it helps to consider your body as separate from you. You have a body—you are not your body. So even if you think your body is a little bit ratty, you can get to know it, slowly, curiously, nonjudgmentally, by caring for it. And it might end up your friend.

Literal interpretation: You do not have to wait to care about your body to care for your body. In fact, caring for your body can often cause you to start liking it more.

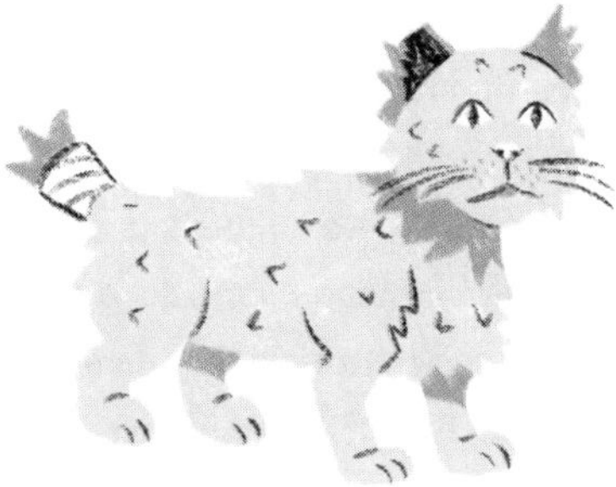

gentle self-talk: "i am allowed to be human"

Someone once commented, "Do you have any suggestions for self-affirmations? I try to do them, but I just don't ever believe them." To be honest, I have conflicting feelings on self-affirmations. During my eighteen months in drug rehab they often told us to look in the mirror and say an affirmation like "I am okay today" or "I am beautiful and people like me." Truth be told, I never felt they helped. I hated myself and saying, "I like myself," in the mirror felt about as effective as saying, "I believe in unicorns"—and about as juvenile. But as I have started down the road of understanding self-compassion, I have found one—just one—affirmation that actually does work for me. And it's this: "I am allowed to be human."

That's it. Humans are born with the birthright of worthiness (thanks, Brené Brown), but you know what? They are also messy, fallible, imperfect creatures who cannot and will not ever get everything right all the time. **And this messy, fallible imperfection never detracts from our inherent worthiness.** I am no exception and neither are you. When I get it wrong or struggle, this simple sentence reminds me that my worthiness is not at stake. So join me next time you feel the panic of making a mistake and say, "I am allowed to be human."

One day I just start asking, "What if I am? What if I am deserving of kindness? What if I am worthy of love? What if I am someone who deserves a functioning space? What if I am allowed to make mistakes?"

It doesn't matter what you think the answer is. Just start making room for the possibility you are wrong when you say you aren't worthy.

good enough is perfect

for several months I have gone to bed with my kitchen clean. The secret? I don't care what my front hallway looks like. It gets to look however it wants. It's none of my business. My clothes always get put up on washday because I stopped caring if they were folded or not. And my bedroom feels serene and tidy because I have given the bathroom permanent permission to look like a feral raccoon lives in it. The secret that is allowing me to have a functional home is that I've been half assing it all. And it's better than it has ever been.

This goes against the grain of what most of us are taught growing up.

Perhaps you grew up hearing the saying "do everything with excellence" (or for those raised religious "do everything to the glory of God!"[6]). And maybe those phrases have fucked you up a little bit. Doing things with excellence doesn't mean doing

---

6   I promise God does not care how you do your laundry.

everything perfectly. If you go through your whole life thinking that every time you clean the fridge it has to be perfect, every time you take a shower it has to be perfect, every time you do a work project it has to be perfect, you will burn out and hate your life. But if prioritizing a few good things that really matter to you and aiming for good enough with the rest of it lets you come out at the end of the day healthy and able to experience joy—now that's an excellent life.

So throw away what you think care tasks "should" look like and work towards a way of doing them that works for *you*. The goal is not to do them to Martha Stewart's standards. Your goal should be to get something functional out of your space. **So while doing a pile of laundry may feel like an accomplishment, it is valid to launder three pairs of underwear as a form of self-care. You have full permission to do a little, do it with shortcuts, and do the bare minimum.** Perfectionism is debilitating. I want you to embrace adaptive imperfection. We aren't settling for less; we are engaging in adaptive routines that help us live and function and thrive. Good enough is perfect.

gentle skill building: changing bedsheets

an old parenting hack is to layer multiple sheets and mattress protectors onto a kid's mattress so that middle-of-the-night accidents are easy to address. Despite knowing this trick, many parents who struggle with getting their own bedsheets changed don't think to try it on themselves. The mattress protector will prevent dirt and sweat from reaching the sheets underneath so you can just pull off the layer and have a clean sheet already on the bed. Even if you do not have or cannot afford multiple mattress covers, layering your sheets onto the bed is a valid way to care for yourself. Getting a new sheet that may have a little bit of sweat on it is more functional than never changing your old sheet. Elevating your functioning is always a good thing. You deserve clean sheets.

rest is a right,
not a reward

If you have been viewing care tasks as moral, it is likely you either a) never stop moving, feel anxious and overwhelmed, and are constantly exhausted or b) lack motivation, feel paralyzed and overwhelmed, and are constantly exhausted. They are really two sides of the same coin. And the coin is shame. When we believe our worth is dependent on completing the never-ending list of care tasks, we are unlikely to let ourselves rest until everything is done. Even when we manage to shame ourselves into action, we find that those who work in shame also rest in shame. Instead of relief, taking a break only brings feelings of guilt. **You do not have to earn the right to rest, connect, or recreate. Unlearn the idea that care tasks must be totally complete before you can sit down.** Care tasks are a never-ending list, and if you wait until everything is done to rest, you will never rest.

Keep in mind that rest is more than sleep. Sleep is a recharging activity that happens when you are unconscious. Tons of studies demonstrate the importance of sleep for your well-being.

We talk less about the equal importance of rest. Rest is a recharging activity that happens when you are conscious. Everyone finds different activities restful, but in general we're seeking the same qualities: connecting, slowing down, and just being, rather than being productive.

Rest is hard for a lot of people because they have conflated "doing nothing" or being unproductive with being lazy. Developing a compassionate inner voice that can challenge these messages is key. Recognize that being nonproductive is a necessary diversion. Rest is necessary for energy, and rest is necessary for work.

As children, many of us are taught we cannot rest or play until our chores are done. This is because our parents desire to teach us the good values of responsibility, delayed gratification, care for our environment, and respect for our family. This arrangement works quite well because as a child your chores are finite. Usually a short list: make your bed, take out the trash, and fold your laundry, et cetera. So we finish this list and move on without guilt. However, when we become adults, this list of care tasks is not finite. It is a never-ending list of tasks that repeat themselves daily. How many of us have internalized the message that we cannot move on to rest or play until this list is done? And if we do, we feel guilt. How will we raise our children (or re-parent ourselves) to learn both responsibility and rest?

Sometimes I come downstairs after putting the kids to bed, look at the house mess, and think, "I really want to sit down, but doing closing duties would be such a kindness to morning me, so I'm going to put on some music and motivate." Other times I come down those stairs and feel the subtle pang of a body and mind asking to be cared for right now—and on those nights I do the bare minimum or even nothing at all. Remember, laziness doesn't exist.

For a long time, when I chose to cut corners with care tasks I would feel immense guilt at being irresponsible. Yet where did I get the message that choosing to prioritize rest over the dishes for one night is irresponsible? The problem isn't that I chose to rest instead of clean the kitchen; it's that I told myself I was being a bad person by doing so. How would it be different if I chose instead to say, "It would be a great kindness to myself right now to just let this go and rest tonight. It will still be there tomorrow"?

Most people fear that if they embrace this type of self-kindness, it will simply enable them to stay unfunctional forever. I think this fear is unfounded.

I don't believe in laziness, but even if I did the good news is that self-kindness is extremely motivating. It might be that when you first start giving yourself full permission to rest without guilt you find yourself resting a lot. Maybe that's what your body and mind need. Research shows that people who report feeling burnout can take months or even years before they start feeling recovered from the damage of that psychological stress. Your body might need that extended time to process and rest and be. If you do this with self-kindness, you will find yourself more motivated to care for yourself than if you pushed on berating yourself for being lazy. So I just wouldn't worry about it. **I find that the balance between rest and work seems to work itself out pretty naturally when you practice self-kindness.**

So whatever you do, friends, do it with kindness.

when you can't financially afford to rest

It's all good and well to beat the drum of rest being vital, but the truth is that some people cannot afford to rest. They have to work constantly just to pay their bills or feed their family. While I know this is true, I have always been too privileged to experience that. So it would be silly of me to try to give advice about how to find times to rest when your hands are full with trying to survive. What I can say is that people who are forced to hustle and grind day in and day out are already some of the most creative and resourceful people I've ever known. They are already, on the regular, having to make decisions between two things they need when they can only afford the time or money for one. Neither I, nor any author, can give a blanket advice that will solve that problem. All I can say is that you absolutely have the right to elevate your need and your family's need for rest as something as deserving of all the creativity and resourcefulness you already have. Maybe that looks like one night a week when everyone eats off paper plates so there are no dishes, and scheduling a family movie night so there is no bedtime struggle and everyone just gets to relax and take it slow. Or maybe it looks completely different for you. There are seasons of life when we just can't get all of our needs met, but the mental shift of seeing rest not as luxury but as a valid need helps you get creative, or at least validates it's okay to mourn how difficult life is right now.

Shortcut: read chapter 25 for a chapter on division of labor or skip to chapter 26.

division of labor:
the rest should be fair

One major burden when it comes to care tasks is dealing with an uneven division of labor in the home between partners. I do not have time to do justice to a complete evaluation of this very valid struggle here. I can, however, offer you a new framework to approach the conversation.

Most couples approach the division of labor from a lens of making the work equal. The formula then should be to quantify how much "work" your paid job is and then quantify how much "work" my paid job is and then dole out the care tasks on top to make it equal between the two.

This approach looks a bit like this:

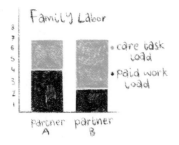

The problem with this approach is that quantifying how much work a task requires isn't an exact science. Deciding who works harder is often a game of apples and oranges. Do you go by hours consumed? What if one job is physically demanding but has shorter hours? How do we compare jobs that are mentally or emotional draining to those that are not? What about those whose jobs create an "on call at all hours" atmosphere? Should someone who travels for work be doing fewer care tasks because they are spending so much time at work or more care tasks because they are doing no joint care tasks at all when they are away?

Most importantly, when I see couples begin to argue from the stance of "who works harder" the discussion is already lost. If the framework is keeping things equal, then when a partner says, "I need you to do more," what the other hears is, "You aren't doing enough." Once feelings of not being appreciated have joined the discussion, we aren't really talking about the dishes anymore. Partners are now operating from fear. Fear of being taken advantage of (since they clearly don't see how much you work) or fear of taking advantage of someone (or being perceived as if you are). This leads to some partners taking on too much, burning out, and becoming resentful and others taking on too little because they no longer trust their partner to look out for them, and feel they won't be cared for unless they take for themselves.

The goal should not be to make the work equal but to ensure that the rest is fair.

Those who think they will escape this conflict by having one partner stay at home are often the most embroiled in it. Imagine a coal miner and the stay-at-home parent. Let's say they agree that one hour of mining coal is more difficult than one hour of caring for children. Therefore, they presume that the partner doing the less difficult work should take on all of the family's care tasks. Their chart looks equal. So what's the problem?

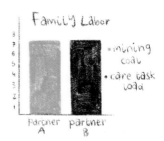

The issue is that in most of these families, the coal miner is getting off work at five and getting two days off a week. Since they have put in their work for the week, they'll feel no issue sleeping in on the weekend and using that time to go and recreate and do what they want. Meanwhile, the partner doing the "easier" job does not have those built-in breaks.

The coal miner and the stay-at-home parent can argue until they are blue in the face about who works harder. The truth is that both are tired. Both want their labor appreciated. And both deserve rest. That's right; even if you have the "easier" job, you still need rest. Care tasks by nature are fundamentally different from paid work. Not harder or easier. Different. They are cyclical and never ending. There is never a moment, especially in the care of children, when everything is "done" and you can clock out. Think of the "easiest" job you can imagine and ask yourself if you would want to work it sixteen hours a day while being on call overnight for 365 days a year. No person can do this and be healthy.

So what would it look like to start the conversation with making the rest fair? For starters, you have two people tasked not with having to prove the value of their work to each other but instead with having to look out for each other, and who ask themselves: How can we ensure we both get rest? This conversation will entail

how to keep house while drowning

who does what around the house, but it will entail so, so much more.

Regardless of whose job is "harder" or "brings in the money," the coal miner is going to need to take on some portion of the care tasks and childcare to create room for their partner to also have times in their week to rest and recreate. True partners will want to do this. They do not view themselves as more entitled to rest than their partner based on paycheck or hours worked. This isn't a business deal where you need to protect your interests against an adversary; it's a partnership where you care about the well-being of each other. This goal is less like the bar graph comparing work and more like a line graph where both work together to ensure rest and enjoyment of life remains fair even as seasons change.

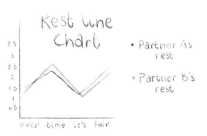

how we hacked fair rest

Michael is a lawyer working at a busy firm. For the first eighteen months of his new career, he worked seven days a week. I was a stay-at-home mom caring for two children. We both deserve rest and we had to figure out a way to ensure our home functioned and we both rested. Here is what we came up with. First, let's get specific about what rest is. Our understanding of rest is as follows:

1. **Rest is fun.** It's a time when you engage in a recreational activity of your choosing. It can be relaxing like watching television or painting (or taking a nap!) or it can be active like hiking or shopping. Rest is not doing care tasks alone. Grocery shopping, getting your hair cut, or taking a shower is not rest.

2. **Rest is recharging.** What you find recharging is unique to you and there are lots of different types of rest. I have friends who find going to a spin class recharging to their mind because the activity helps their mind go blank. This is mentally restful to them. I tend to experience exercise as both physical and mental work and not restful. You may feel most rested when you get alone time to binge-watch your favorite show. I often find stimulating conversation with a good friend over a child-free lunch recharging and socially restful.

3. **Rest includes time autonomy.** Care tasks should be divided in such a way that there is time for everyone to rest and keep the home functioning. In partnerships with children, rest times likely have to be more structured—looking more like protected times in the week when you can decide what you will do without having to "get someone to cover." A situation where one partner can come and go

on a whim and assume the other will care for the children, but the other partner has to practically file HR paperwork with their spouse three weeks ahead of time in order to leave for an afternoon is not a partnership with fair rest. Everyone deserves a window of their week when they have time autonomy.

4. **Rest isn't being on call.** This means that getting to watch a TV show on a Saturday while your kids play in the living room and come in to ask you for snacks and to referee fights every ten minutes is not rest.

5. **Rest includes responsibilities.** It is your partner's responsibility to protect your rest time but your responsibility to actually rest. If your own perfectionism has you using your rest times to scrub baseboards, that is not your partner's fault.

What I am not saying is that watching television while your kids are in the living room isn't fun or that it's not important to get the space to take a shower alone. What I am saying is that those activities do not meet the vital human need for rest.

You'll remember earlier in the chapter I said that rest is more than sleep. This is true. But rest is not less than sleep either. Which is why our goal of equal rest started with sleep. Shortly after our first was born, Michael and I began to divide up our weekend days to ensure we both got sleep. On Saturday mornings I wake up early with the kids, and on Sunday mornings he does. The sleeping partner gets until 10:00 am to either sleep in or presumably wake and do whatever they want (we've always chosen to sleep). Michael often has to work at least some hours on the weekend and it's understood that I am holding down the fort while he does that. However, we have an understanding that non–sleeping or working hours during the weekend are assumed to be family co-parenting hours. No one just walks out the door to go to whatever assuming the other will watch the kids. Instead, we game plan what we need or would like to get done that weekend by way of both obligation and fun. It's not about getting permission; it's about giving respect. Free time does not automatically belong to one parent at the expense of the other.

In the evenings when Michael comes home from work, he rolls right into engaging our children. I will pivot from the children to making dinner and then he does bath time and bedtime while I do closing duties (more on those later). We both finish up around 7:30 pm and sit down to watch television with each other until bedtime.

Oftentimes when we sit down at 7:30 the living room is a mess, the laundry is unfolded, and at least one area of our house looks like a bomb went off. Yet we sit down anyways. Everyone clocks out at 7:30 pm. That's because the key to ensuring fair rest in our home has much more to do with showing appreciation and giving each other the benefit of the doubt than it does with whose job it is to take out the trash. How we speak to each other, enjoy each other, and love each other in the million non–care task spheres of our lives sets a foundation of trust. Michael doesn't wake up early to get kids ready for the day and that's fine with me; I assume that means he needs the extra sleep. Likewise, our home is never picture-perfect when he comes home and that's just fine with him; he assumes that means the kids and I must have had either a really fun or really difficult day.

Michael and I are not without our normal marital struggles. Like all couples, we have disagreements on family labor at times. But it has still served us best to focus on striving for the rest being fair. Fair rest covers a multitude of division of labor sins.

gentle skill building: bathrooms

there are seasons of life when the goal of cleaning is to figure out how to get the most amount of function from the least amount of energy. There is a finite amount of energy and hours in the day, and I guess you could spend that time taking a cleaning task from good enough to great. But why would you? When you've self-actualized and you've got extra time you can do that.

Until then, just get two Clorox wands with the disposable heads and use one to clean the toilet and the other to clean the shower, the tub, and the sink. Wipe the counters and the shower door and the mirrors with Windex and some paper towels. You're doing fine. Absolutely no one is going to be lying on their deathbed with regrets about not cleaning their bathroom enough.

A note for survivors of abuse:

If the abuse you endured involved humiliation, degradation, shaming, or sexual acts, it can be very difficult to clean toilets.

Putting your face in the place where genitals go and excrement happens can be very triggering. If that is the case for you, be very gentle with yourself. If it's very difficult for you, you can pass this task off to someone else in your home or pay someone else to do it.

gentle skill building: a system for keeping your car clean

i dunno, friends. My car looks like shit. I don't have this one figured out. I may never have this one figured out. That's okay too. I honestly stopped putting much effort into trying. This journey isn't about some mythical destination where everything has the perfect system; it's about permission to make things functional and permission to enjoy your life even if your car never gets clean.

when your body doesn't cooperate

Sometimes the barrier to getting care tasks done isn't your mind but your body. Your mind wants to, but your body feels like it has sand sacks for legs. Maybe it's because you were up all night. Maybe it's chronic illness or pain or pregnancy. Maybe you're going through a situation in your life that's extremely stressful and it's affecting you physically. It's times like this when racing the clock or playing motivation games don't really help. **What does help is to just let yourself move as slowly as you need to.** No timers. No agenda. You may not get it all done. But you get more done than you would've if you hadn't done anything. Below is an inexhaustive list of products and routines that may be helpful to you:

- Grabbers for picking things off the floor without bending
- Rolling office chairs or stools for moving about the house for care tasks

- A shower chair for showering without fatigue
- Cleaning caddies and supplies for each room or floor to reduce having to walk
- Three-tier cart for supplies to roll around instead of carry
- A long-handled dustpan
- An automatic scrubber attachment for drill
- Sweeping or using a rake to gather items on the floor into a pile so you can sit down to sort them out
- Doing only a commercial-worth of time while watching a show to pace yourself
- Timing to stay within safe exertion limits
- Installing grab bars in bathrooms or other high fall risk areas
- Doubling or tripling recipes to freeze for hard days
- A "gentle movement" playlist of slow songs to help you move slowly while you work

contributing is morally neutral

When you experience legitimate barriers to completing care tasks while living in a partnership with someone else, you may experience guilt. Even those who have understanding partners experience this from time to time. Let's explore what is morally neutral about contributing to a family.

I believe the moral gut check here isn't "Am I contributing enough?" but "Am I taking advantage of someone else?"

You are not required to contribute to be worthy of love and care and belonging. We know this is true because you could be connected to a ventilator unable to contribute anything (and in fact be using lots of resources) and still be a worthy human being. We all have seasons of life when we are capable of contributing more or less than the people around us.

This is a hard concept to tease out because there are some very obviously wrong ways to act when it comes to division of household labor. A partner who comes home after work and expects to relax all evening while their partner, who also worked all day (whether inside or outside the home), does all of the house-hold labor is clearly in the wrong and should feel guilty. But the moral issue is not that that partner is not contributing enough—it's that they feel more entitled to rest than their partner and are exploiting their partner's labor to get it. If you feel more entitled to more respect because of your gender or the size of your paycheck, that is wrong.

This is what I try to teach my children when we talk about care tasks in our home. Instead of telling them that contributing is a moral obligation, I place the value on our attitudes towards one another. I want my kids to be responsible, yes. But just as important, I want them to know that it's okay to not "pull their weight" when they are sick with the flu. I want my kids to grow up to care for others and treat them fairly without being crushed by the false guilt of thinking their worth is tied to how much they can produce or contribute. I want that for all of us.

Summary: Contribution and productivity are not moral values—but nonexploitation and humility are. When someone demands the benefits of being a part of a family but refuses responsibilities to that family of which they are capable, it's a form of entitlement that exploits the other members of that family. However, having a limited capacity is not the same as being entitled and accepting help is not the same as exploiting others.

cleaning and parental trauma

"**m**y dad used to come home late at night and if the house wasn't spotless he would wake us up screaming and make us clean in the middle of the night. I was always so tired the next day at school."

"My mother would lock me in my room and tell me to clean it. I was so overwhelmed by the mess I would just sit there paralyzed and she would come in and scream at me for being lazy."

"If I didn't clean my room to their standards, they would come in and dump everything on the floor and tell me to start over."

These are just a few of the examples of chore trauma I've heard from clients. It is not uncommon for abusive caregivers to use chores as a manner of punishment and humiliation, as a way to withhold love and inflict pain. This has a profound impact on the little self, and the messaging carries into adulthood. This usually has one of two effects: (1) you avoid care tasks because you see them as punishment and now that you are an adult you can finally get free of them, or (2) you are constantly and even obsessively cleaning because you have internalized the message that you are dirty or failing if anything is out of place. Next time you hear the inner bully, pay close attention to the messages it gives. Is it really your voice, or is it the voice of a past caregiver? Therapy can be a huge help in unpacking this type of trauma and can help you redefine care tasks as care instead of punishment.

If you experienced neglect and abuse as a child and that abuse happened in a very dirty or cluttered environment, you may feel it is your utmost duty as a parent to never let your kids feel the way you did as a child. It's important to remember that your children do not have the same emotional context around mess or dirt as you. Mess to you was chaos and danger. It was a lack of safety, and being unloved and uncared for. No parent wants their children to feel this way, which is why you may go overboard ensuring there is never any mess or clutter—maybe even to the point of exhaustion or emotional distress. Let me offer you some comfort. **Your children will never experience mess the way you did if *you* are safe and loving.** Toys on the floor will mean nothing to them but a parent who cared enough to buy them. Dishes in the sink will represent to them a parent who always fed them. Stains on their clothes will remind them of how cool it is to have a parent who lets them use art supplies or play in the mud.

Tear this out and hang it in your home:

"This is a safe home and I am safe in it."

This is a safe home and I am safe in it.

critical family members

even as we become comfortable giving ourselves kindness and compassion in the midst of struggle, we often still have to contend with friends or family members who are at different parts of the journey of moral neutrality. How do we respond when someone criticizes the state of our home or tries to "help" us by giving advice that doesn't really fit?

My favorite phrase for well-meaning family is, "I know you want to see me in a functioning environment and I want you to know that I want that for myself also. I am on my own journey to find what works for me and what I need most from you is nonjudgmental support. One thing that could really help me right now is _____."

And then give them a tangible task they can do! "Take these bags of clothes to the donation bin," "sit with me while I clean my room," "help me call a cleaning service or make a doctor's appointment." Sometimes all our loved ones need is to be redirected to a way they can actually help. If after you give them ways to help they decline, it's okay to say, "Then the most helpful thing you can do for me is not make comments about my space."

If you have a particularly rude or pushy person in your life, you can use my favorite boundary phrase, which is "thank you for your concern, but I am not taking any feedback on this issue right now." ☺

Or my personal favorite: "The key for me being able to begin to run a functioning home was when I stopped talking to myself the way you are talking to me right now."

Shortcut: skip to chapter 33.

rhythms over routines

dr. Lesley Cook, a brilliant psychologist who works with ADHD, once said to me, "Forget about creating a routine. You have to focus on finding your rhythm."

With routines you are either on track or not. With rhythm you can skip a beat and still get back in the groove.

I used to try to do things as they looked like they needed to be done—changing the sheets when they looked dirty, running the dishwasher when it was full, doing laundry when I ran out of clean clothes. Except what actually happened was I would notice the sheets were dirty and then get around to changing them a month later, avoid the sink of dishes because it was overwhelming, and load up the laundry and forget it in the washer for three days and have to run it again. One problem was I was usually in the middle of doing something when I was noticing some care tasks that were "ready" to be addressed, which left me the options of saying either, "Oh, I'll do that later," and forgetting, or, "I better do that now so I don't forget" and then forgetting the thing I was already in the middle of doing. I felt like I was constantly being pulled in a bunch of different directions and never actually having a home that functioned.

I was serving my home, but my home wasn't serving me. I needed to change that. So I put the house on my schedule. As a mom and a neurodivergent person I've learned that I do well with daily and weekly rhythms. So I started doing laundry every Monday even when there were still clean clothes left, washing the sheets every Thursday even if they weren't "too dirty," and running my dishwasher every night even if it wasn't full. Sure, I was doing things a little more often or at times less often than they "should" be done, but who cares? **The best way to do something is the way it gets done.**

rituals

If you are someone who can walk into a messy room and just start picking up random items and putting them away like some kind of freaking wizard, I am truly happy for you. I am not like that. I will wander around feeling overwhelmed for twenty minutes and then give up. Or I'll start picking up random items only to hold them or set them somewhere else they don't go before getting sucked into some tiny project that doesn't matter like organizing my yarn collection.

Then I learned to work with my brain instead of against it. **I came up with rituals that outlined exactly what I was to do in a room and exactly in what order.** My Five Things Tidying Method is one such ritual. Closing duties is another. This allows me to hyperfocus on whatever list item I'm on like I'm on SEAL Team 6 or a character in a video game. There are all sorts of silly games I play with myself. Sometimes I narrate in my head like I'm a world-renowned cleaning expert and everyone is watching me on television. This lets me block out everything else and gives me a way forward so my brain can go on autopilot. By virtually eliminating the decision-making of where to start or what to do next I can move from task to task with virtually no time in between. The momentum it creates circumvents a lot of executive functioning issues I experience.

new habits and systems

When you want to introduce some new habits or systems into your home to make things a bit more functional, don't shoot for the moon. Go for the closest to what you're already doing with a little bit of increased function. Here are some examples:

If you tend to toss clothes into a certain chair all day, instead of saying, "That's it! From now on everything goes straight to the laundry room," try just putting a laundry basket next to the chair and putting things into the laundry basket instead. Now you can take the whole basket to the laundry room when you can and it looks a little more contained until then.

If you tend to leave dishes everywhere, instead of saying, "From now on I'm going to wash every dish as soon as I use it," instead try taking dishes to the sink when you're done and just leaving them in there. Once a system becomes easy and automatic you can try another little tweak to increase the function even more. For example, maybe instead of putting the dishes into the sink you stack them up in categories on the side of the sink so that your sink is accessible.

If a system never becomes easy or automatic for you, then

it just means either the system isn't the right one for you or you need more tips and tools to get the system to work. The issue is never that you are failing or not good enough.

momentum over perfection

Two years ago I vowed to never do another diet or ever exercise from a motive of wanting to lose weight or be thinner. And so for two years I didn't exercise. This past year, I finally felt a genuine desire to move my body, both for the pleasure of movement and for the health benefits. It's a very different experience. For one, I'm really bad at it. I can only do it for very short periods. In the past, when I only exercised for the aesthetic benefits, my inability to do enough to lose weight was overwhelming and caused me to quit. These days, I find myself doing five minutes here and ten minutes there of the most low-impact exercise I can manage and instead of that being a failure in my eyes because it's not enough to produce weight loss it has been a success because I know every minute is giving my body and mind a functional benefit. I've also come to realize that anything that creates momentum is a win. The momentum of getting on the exercise bike from time to time keeps me feeling as though I have the momentum to get myself on the exercise bike from time to time. It's becoming a part of my rhythm. It may not be a fast-paced regular rhythm, it's more like a slow, erratic jazz rhythm, but the momentum is there.

Creating momentum is key because motivation builds motivation. Having a goal of momentum is great because it frees you to start with tasks that actually matter to you. For example, when it was difficult for me to find the motivation to do dishes or laundry I felt as though that should be the first thing to tackle. But what I did first was start putting slippers next to my bed at night. I realized that whenever I wake up in the morning and my feet are cold as I walk to the bathroom it was not only a super unpleasant experience, but it was also one I could rectify pretty easily. Is it a big deal? No. Is it silly to start with something so superficial when I could just suck it up and do what "really" matters? I don't think so. When I started putting those slippers next to my bed at night it made those few morning minutes so pleasant that I actually felt an organic motivation to do it again the next night. You might think being cold for a few minutes in the morning should be a much lower priority than finding a way to get your dishes and laundry done, but motivation builds motivation. We are learning to flex the muscles of motivation and rhythm and ritual.[7] **Practicing a care task you directly experience as actual care, like putting** **a pair of slippers by your bed at night, can help you get the motivation to do the other things as well.** I'm not suggesting you try putting slippers by your bed—what you choose to practice on will be unique to what's important to you. I'm also not saying it has to be a lifelong habit—just one to practice with for a bit. What is one thing you could do for yourself today that would be truly enjoyable for tomorrow you?

---

7 "Flexing the muscles of motivation" is another way of saying we are going to practice this skill until it seems easier to us.

gentle skill building: maintaining a space

a simple plan to keep a space livable is better than an overwhelming plan to keep a space perfect. One of the easiest ways
to do this is to look at one space in your home you would like to
keep livable. Perhaps this is your bedroom or the kitchen. If you
are a parent, you might pick a child's room or playroom. Think of
four to six tasks that, if they were done every week, would make
that space very livable. For example, let's say I look around my
bedroom and decide that (1) if the cups and dishes were taken
out, (2) if the sheets were changed, (3) if the laundry was thrown
into the washer and started, and (4) if trash was thrown away
and taken out, it would be a very livable space. You might decide
to repeat some twice a week. Then decide which part of your
day is most routine and add doing that one thing to your routine.
Perhaps most days you get ready for work or every day at noon
you put kiddos down for a nap. Hang the list in the room so you
can see it and complete your task. When I did this to my daughter's bedroom, I decided that if the diapers and trash were taken

out of her room and her crib sheets were changed, then even if the whole day fell to shit I could still feel good about taking care of her space. This was a powerful first step for me.

cleaning schedules

The previous example is a great starting point for maintenance when you feel overwhelmed. Some people like the idea of a weekly cleaning schedule and have the lifestyle that allows for that sort of thing each day. This is neither necessary nor superior to cleaning ad hoc or waiting until you have a large chunk of time to knock out several things—but some might prefer it. As a stay-at-home parent, I played around with the idea of a cleaning schedule—trying to do one cleaning task each day so things didn't become overwhelming. I used one chart for the upstairs and one for the downstairs. When I began to work again, the daily tasks didn't seem to get done anymore, so I shifted to a slightly longer list that I would do on Sunday afternoons. Regardless of how (or even if) you schedule your cleaning, I suggest writing these three "rules" down where you can see them:

1. **This list is here to serve me; I do not serve this list.** This schedule is here to make my life easier, not to make it harder. The schedule isn't for telling me what I must do or reminding me about what I haven't done. The way it serves me each day is by taking the burden of decision-making away. I don't have to

feel as though I have to clean everything and I don't have to waste time analyzing which task should be prioritized. I get to do the thing for today and then focus on other things knowing I'll get to the rest of it eventually.

2. **Missing days is morally neutral.** I can miss days or decide to do something different anytime I want or need to. Confession: I have never once followed through on the dusting day on my schedule.

3. **I do not have to complete the whole task.** I have more than one bathroom in my house. I don't ever clean all of them in a day. I simply pick the one I think needs cleaning, or the most convenient one, or even the one I did last week because I don't want to spend very much time on it. I'll get to them all eventually and even if they are dirty some of the time if I'm always doing something it will always look better than it was. Most days that read "clean kitchen" I just pick a few things to clean in the kitchen. Perhaps I wipe down the counters and clean the microwave one week; the next week I'll do the stove. This approach means I always feel good that I am caring for my space and avoid the anxiety that makes me feel as though I am a servant to the list.

monthly tasks

For larger household maintenance, choose between six and twelve tasks (you may want some tasks to be done twice a year). Below are some suggestions. Assign each task a month. Remember, while there are a lot of suggestions out there on how often to do these things, there is no universal right way. The right way for you is anything that keeps your space functional without overwhelming you. You may be tempted to add several things to each month. If you are already in the habit of doing several things each month, then go for it. However, if you are just starting out it may be best to stick with one and see how it goes. Some items on this list may simply not matter to you and that's okay. Some may seem like too much for you and it's okay to skip those items. It's better to have a low-key home care plan that you feel empowered to do than a perfect one that is left undone or adds stress to your life. Don't forget you can always ask or pay for help with these items. Having a plan allows you to predict and prepare.

- Change the AC filter
- Clean out kitchen cabinets
- Clean out the garage
- Purge closet and donate old clothes
- Purge and donate toys
- Clean inside of refrigerator
- Pack in or out seasonal clothes
- Clean inside of garbage can
- Clean gutters

what to do when you can't get the list done

When I began a little cleaning schedule, I noticed there was an item I kept doing inconsistently or skipping altogether. I would then feel bad for not doing the whole weekly list. So I came up with a hack for ensuring the whole list would get done.

I took that item off the list. Now the whole list gets done.

"But KC!" you say. "The item you took off isn't getting done now." Well, it wasn't getting done when it was on the list either, only now I don't feel guilty about it. It just goes back to being randomly done when I think about it and I still have a functioning closing duty list. Leaning into the things we feel naturally motivated to do creates momentum. The momentum of turning the care cycles every day is like a car engine. It creates its own charge.[8] If you keep the momentum going, you're more likely to get the random task you took off the list done one day anyways.

(PS: It was the dusting day.)

restock day

You know what I hate? I hate having to bring dish towels downstairs from the laundry. I hate having to replace toilet paper. I hate having to refill the upstairs diaper station. I really dislike any small and tedious task like this. But I also hate not having dish towels

---

8   In other words, motivation literally creates more motivation.

when I need them, or toilet paper, or diapers. I know my life is so much more functional when these little tasks are done, but I just loathe them. They are never in the flow. I usually notice them while I'm in the middle of doing something else. **When I realized it was the tiresome interruptions I hated, I compiled as many of these small restocking tasks in to one big task: Restock Day.** And because I had long since quit trying to dust every Tuesday I had an opening. This put the restock into the flow. I put on some music, I get my list out, and I accomplish a task in a way that actually feels productive.

it doesn't happen all at once

It took me over a year to get some basic systems in place that helped my house function. And I'm not done yet. Sometimes we think, "When I'm done and it's all in order, then I'll be able to breathe and I won't feel this way," but the reality is there is no finish line. And that's a good thing. You don't have to do better to start feeling better. You can start a journey of creating functional systems for you while being kind to yourself. You deserve kindness regardless of how many working systems you've found. Even if that kindness is only coming from yourself. You can live a joyful life and be just good enough at care tasks, even if things aren't totally functional yet. It's a process and one that I am still in too. The key is to embrace that idea that there is no finish line of worthiness. You are worthy now. There is only increased function ahead. And it's going to be wonderful.

my favorite ritual: closing duties

remember when you did the exercise of being kind to little you? Well, now I am going to talk more about being kind to future you. Anyone who has worked in the service industry is familiar with opening and closing duties. Servers and bartenders have "side duties" in addition to serving customers that help get the restaurant open and set the next shift up for success. Openers will cut lemons, set tables, polish wineglasses, and start the coffee. At the end of their shift, they will clean the tables, restock the salt and pepper, and roll silverware. Closers will put the plates away, clean the booths, and disinfect the soda machine. Side duties are not the servers' "main job," but they must get done in order for servers to do their main job of waiting tables.

I've already talked about how, when you have the opportunity to do a task and struggle with the motivation to start it, it might be helpful to think you are doing it as a kindness to "future you." What does future you need to function tomorrow? On a good day, I like to unload and reload my dishwasher, pick up some toys, pack kid lunches for the morning, throw away whatever trash is lying around, take my medication, and make cold-brew coffee for the morning. **It only takes about thirty minutes to do these little closing duties, but I know it's going to make future KC have an easier time functioning tomorrow.**

The power in closing duties is the power of permission. Permission to care for tomorrow you without having to make things perfect or up to other people's standards. But closing duties are only powerful if you also have permission to not do them. The key is that while doing them is a way of taking care of tomorrow you, sometimes not doing them is a way of taking care of right now you. That's why I have a survival day list. Sometimes I'm sick or stressed. Other times I could be having a perfectly great day and abruptly at 4:00 pm feel like I've hit a brick wall. When that happens the priority becomes getting my kids to bed with kindness. For those days we have survival closing duties. What's the bare minimum I need to function tomorrow? Clean baby bottles, throw food waste away so it doesn't spoil, and take my medication. So I open up my dishwasher full of clean dishes, take three bowls out and put the dirty baby bottles in their place, and run it again. I throw food wrappers away to prevent bugs, and I take my medication. It takes five minutes, and the motivation is kindness, kindness to both right now KC and tomorrow KC. Then I sit down and watch television and hang out with my husband. It's a true win-win situation: right now me gets to rest and future me gets to function.

Timing: I do my closing duties right after I feed my kids dinner. I put my youngest to sleep because I can lay her in the crib and walk right out, and while Michael puts our older daughter to sleep (the longer and more labor-intensive of the two bedtime jobs) I walk downstairs and roll right into closing duties. If I sit down and relax first, it becomes very difficult to get up again. Butting your closing duties up against another activity where you are already up can be key. I typically wrap up around the time Michael gets done with bedtime and I officially clock out for the night.

don't forget: momentum is key!

Here is what to do if you find yourself not doing your closing duties list: (1) Make a shorter list. Even if there is just one thing on it. (2) Change what is on the list. If you have things on there you think you are "supposed" to do but don't really care about, of course you will not feel motivated. Put something on there you really care about. Maybe you *should* do the dishes every night so you don't get bugs. But maybe you actually care about having coffee ready to brew first thing in the morning. (3) Change the timing of when you do closing duties. Perhaps it works better if you do them right as you walk in the door from work. Don't even take off your shoes; just roll right into it. Maybe doing them as opening duties suits you better because you have more energy and motivation then. This isn't about doing what you are supposed to; it's about being kind to yourself. You can grow and change the list once you have gained momentum.

skill deficit versus support deficit

q uit beating yourself up for having a skill deficit when what you really have is a support deficit. **Self-care was never meant to be a replacement for community care.**[9] Striving to "be better" will exhaust the little energy you have, and it's probably time better spent letting yourself cry and sleep and finding small pockets of joy to keep you going. A support deficit is not always someone's fault. There are just some seasons of life we have to limp through.

I so often look back on these seasons of limping through and say to myself with tenderness, "Wow, I was really doing the best I could with what I had." And that's the funny thing about doing your best; it never *feels* like your best at the time. In fact, it almost always feels like failing when you're in it. When I look back at sixteen-year-old me in rehab, sobbing alone and feel-

---

9   Take a look at the history behind the term self-care sometime. Start with googling Audre Lorde. It wasn't always about yoga and hobbies.

ing worthless, constantly being told I wasn't making enough progress, I see now she was doing her best. I sometimes wish someone at the time could have seen it and told me so. But that's okay. I tell her myself now all the time.

outsourcing care tasks is morally neutral

If you can afford a housekeeper, even once a month, and you do not have one, you must ask yourself why. Do you think you deserve one? Why not? Housekeepers are not moral and therefore are not something to be deserved. If you are in a season of life when there are simply more care tasks to be done than time or energy available to you and you have the means to afford help, it is the most functional thing to do. Does embarrassment stop you? "I could never let a housekeeper see the state of my home" is about as logical as "I could never let a doctor see the state of my health." And so what if the housekeeper judges you? It is not their mental health you are responsible for but your own. One route that I might suggest is to skip the cleaning services and instead find an individual through a website like care.com or a local Facebook group. When you work with an individual, you have more control over what you would like to have done and how much time you want them to spend doing it.

For the first several months of my youngest daughter's life, I was completely underwater with quarantine and postpartum depression. When she turned eight months old, I made the decision to get some help. I hired a grad student to come clean a couple hours a week for an hourly wage for about two months. I told her frankly that she may walk in some days to everything being a disaster. I said what I needed might change from week to week. I told her she may not even finish some weeks but that making a dent in the mess would go a long way. When she arrived, I had her fold the mass of clean laundry on the floor that had piled up during the week (this was before my no-folding system), then clean either the upstairs or the downstairs depending on what I felt I needed or wanted that week. It was the best experience with a cleaning "service" I ever had. In the past when I had a cleaning service, I would feel stressed out at having to pre-clean and pick up before they got there. Knowing I didn't have to do that took so much stress away. Because I knew she would be there for a set amount of time, every week I found myself taking the time to pick up and doing a little cleaning so I could get the most out of her help. Interestingly enough, the subtle shift from obligation to option created motivation for me.

If you cannot afford to pay for help with care tasks, consider asking family or friends. Sometimes just having someone to keep you company while you complete tasks is helpful. If you have a friend who struggles with certain care tasks, you can form a little co-op where you go to your house one week and help each other clean or do laundry and then do the other person's house the next week.

Sometimes we come from a cultural-familial background that

says only pretentious people hire help for those sorts of things. The truth is that it's no more pretentious to pay someone to clean your home than it is to pay someone to change the oil in your car. If it's something that would make your functioning easier and you can afford it, that's the only criterion. **Whether it's hiring a cleaning service, meal delivery, curbside groceries, or using a wash and fold, as long as you treat people with respect and pay them what they are worth, it's all morally neutral.**

Remember, feeling ashamed to pay for help is often directly related to the idea that care tasks are moral obligations central to your worthiness as a human. Paid domestic help is not a prescription. You don't have to meet a diagnostic criterion to deserve to hire someone to help you with domestic tasks any more than you have to meet a criterion to not have to churn your own butter or knit your own sweaters.

Shortcut: read on for topics of exercise, weight, and food or skip to chapter 41.

exercise sucks

I blame PE class as the first offender. I really do. At such an early age kids who love to play active games are made to run laps instead. Okay, maybe that isn't every school, but it was certainly the first time I remember someone divorcing physical activity from fun and creating the demon that is exercise. Then diet culture came along and told us the reason we should be engaging this exercise is primarily to keep our bodies thin and attractive.

These things have really wrecked our relationship to joyful body movement. If you are motivated to an activity by body shame, experience the activity as a chorus of unpleasant sensory experiences (pain, boredom, and sweat are my three *least* favorite things in the world), and then end with no immediate results, *why on earth would you like that activity or want to do it ever again?*

So I stand by my statement. Exercise, as it currently exists in most of our lives, sucks. Like most care tasks, when they function only to fulfill external standards of what we should be doing, it actually moves us further away from real care for self.

But when I look back at my life and ask myself, "What memories of movement do I have that are joyful?" I well up with tears. I remember cheerleading in the eighth grade and feeling so happy as my body hit every beat on point and in sync with the rest of my team. I remember jumping higher than I think any human has as we won second place in a championship. I remember how strong I felt that I could throw a girl in the air.

I remember youth soccer games and the absolute rush it gave me to feel my foot connect with power to the ball.

I remember dancing stoned out of my mind at a Bob Marley festival, barefoot and uncaring that my body moved like a jellyfish, oblivious to the beat or how it should be moving.

I remember, at ten years sober, when my wedding DJ dedicated "Rehab" by Amy Winehouse to all of us who had come through hell and survived and an entire dance floor of little sober assholes absolutely went nuts on the dance floor. I remember Josh splitting his pants. I remember my husband looking at me like no other woman existed. I remember being carried over the threshold of our hotel that night, not out of tradition, but because I had worn the bottoms of my feet raw dancing.

When did movement lose its pleasure? When did my adult life stop including activities that made movement joyful? Can I get it back? Can you? Can we try together?

your weight is morally neutral

feeding your body is a care task. Resting your body is a care task. Taking medication to control health symptoms is a care task. Moving your body is a care task. Physical therapy and other healing activities are care tasks. It's a wonderful thing to investigate what foods and nutrients help your body function and feel best. But making or keeping yourself thin is not a care task.

There are lots of ways to make your body smaller that will not produce better health. I'm neither a doctor nor a dietician, but I've listened to tons of these providers who practice from a Health at Every Size standpoint. These providers can help you introduce healthy habits into your life that will make you feel better and function better without focusing on making your body smaller. When we begin to care for our body with those types of care tasks, sometimes we lose weight, sometimes we gain weight, and sometimes our weight doesn't change at all. Your weight is morally neutral. The weight you are after you adopt healthy habits into your life is the weight you are supposed to be.

I recently had someone comment on a video of mine saying, "You'd look better if you lost weight." My first thought was, "Look better to who?" because I don't feel any obligation to produce sexual attractiveness for some rando on the internet. The comment stayed with me for days though, not because it hurt my feelings but because I was surprised that it didn't.

One night I was lying in bed and cuddling my eighteen-month-old. She was asleep in my arms with her angelic face resting in the crook of my elbow. We were lying next to my husband, a man whom I love deeply and who loves me. On the floor on a little pallet was my three-year-old, a spitfire little sprite who brightens my world. I realized that I only ever wanted to be skinny because I wanted to be loved and happy. But I already have that. Skinny hasn't seemed very important to me since then.

food is morally neutral

You deserve to eat.

Nothing you ate yesterday, said today, or have left undone for tomorrow can take away your right to be fed. Your inability to create a nutritiously perfect meal today does not mean your body is better off not eating. All calories are good calories when you're having a hard time. There are no good or bad foods. There are no right or wrong foods. And I'm gonna say it: there are no foods that are absolutely healthy or unhealthy. Healthy is a wholistic state of being that requires more than just knowing the amount and type of nutrients in the food you are eating. Being kind to yourself while eating ice cream is healthier than hating yourself while eating a salad. Anxiety and perfectionism are not good for your health. At the end of the day, your relationship to food is as much a factor in your health as fueling your body in a way that makes you feel good is.

Meal planning is not a thing people who have it all together do. Meal planning exists to make it easier for you to eat and buy groceries. That is the function. For most of my life, meal planning caused way more stress than not knowing what to eat did. So I didn't do it. Once I had a family of four, that flipped and it became more stressful to stare at the fridge with little sentient leg weights hanging on to my ankles, so I started trying to plan what was going to be for dinner that week ahead of time. There is no right way here; it's simply what is the lower stress option. You get to decide.

If you would like to try meal planning, it helps to first de-Pinterest the idea. If you eat a meal and you like it, write it down. Start a list. They don't have to be intricate, cohesive meals either. Eat a really good sandwich? Write it down. Pour some jar sauce over some tortellini and it hit the spot? Onto the list it goes. Eventually, you'll have a list of meals you like. Before going to the grocery store you can pick out a few for the week. Voila. You meal planned.

If feeding yourself is very hard, turn your attention to kids' food. Toddler food is designed to shotgun the maximum amount of nutrients into someone with a limited palate and an even more limited attention span. Yogurt pouches, Uncrustables, microwave macaroni and cheese . . . throw in a multivitamin and you'll live to see another day.

getting back into rhythm

even as my journey to hack the house started making care tasks easier for me, I still had days when I just . . . couldn't. After a particularly long stretch of no preschool, one of my kids got sick and I woke up feeling completely fatigued and unable to motivate. We stayed in our pj's, watched *Trolls* five times, and I put us all to bed (myself included) at 7:00 pm.

I woke up the next morning feeling rested and ready to have a day that was more organized. I felt motivated and able to do some care tasks that day and even catch up on what was left undone from the previous day. A big part of that was how I chose to speak to myself about the day before. If I viewed a day of screen time and not doing any scheduled care tasks as a failure, it would be a lot harder to "get back into routine." But I didn't. *Trolls* and pj's day was a day when we were being gentle with ourselves, allowing ourselves to take it easy and rest—a day of kindness. Framing it as kindness instead of failure was the key to being able to wake up and choose to get things done the next day.

you deserve a
beautiful sunday

I recently got a comment from a follower that said: "Thank you! I'm spending the day outside enjoying our beautiful weather and getting a pumpkin coffee instead of doing my usual 8-hour Sunday clean. It's so not necessary. I will instead do a 2-hour clean when I get home." It made me want to do a happy dance! She nailed it. Yes, if we want to go enjoy a beautiful Sunday, we will need clothes to wear. That's the benefit of having some laundry done. Our body will need to be able to have the strength and energy to carry us during our beautiful Sunday activities, and that's the benefit of feeding it. You may want to wear your new hat or read a book at the park, and that's the benefit of a space that allows you to find what you need. All of these things are functional, not moral. You do not need to complete eight hours of care tasks in order to deserve a day at the park. You can enjoy your day and then spend two hours bringing things into functional order so you can enjoy your upcoming week as well. **That is the life-changing result of internalizing that**

you do not exist to serve your space, your space exists to serve you.

Care tasks exist for one reason only . . . to make your body and space functional enough for you to easily experience the joy this world has to offer.

acknowledgments

a huge thanks to all those who made this book possible. To Kimberly Witherspoon, Jessica Mileo, and everyone else at InkWell Management who believed in me, to Leah Trouwborst and the team at Simon & Schuster who supported my vision from the beginning, and to all the friends and family who let me run ideas by them and read early excerpts of the book, especially my sweet husband, Michael, who edited the self-published edition of *How to Keep House While Drowning* in his spare time while being a new attorney; Rachel Moulton, who gave freely of her time and expertise as an author when I knew nothing about the industry; my mother-in-law, Debbie Phipps, for connecting us; and my own mom, for being one of the first people to tell me that I really had something worth pursuing when I first began my platform.

There is a special debt of gratitude owed to Imani Barbarin, for reading the manuscript with an eye for inclusivity that my privileges tend to blind me to; Dr. Raquel Martin, for her contributions to my understanding of Afro-textured-hair care; and Robin

Roscigno, for her feedback on how best to create a book that neurodivergent communities could read easily. Their contributions and feedback on how, make this book inclusive beyond just my own communities and privileges.

I would like to acknowledge Dr. Brené Brown and Dr. Kristin Neff as profound influences on my work, as their research on shame and self-compassion, respectively, has been foundational for me. I would also like to acknowledge Caroline Dooner, whose book *The F*ck It Diet* introduced me to the Intuitive Eating principles of food and body neutrality, a concept that springboarded me into questioning what other aspects of my life were neither good nor bad, and Lesley Cook, PsyD, who has contributed so much to my understanding of executive functioning and how best to help those who struggle with it.

Acknowledgment and thanks are also owed to every black woman involved in the natural hair movement, which brought curly hair care to my attention and introduced me to how helpful silk bonnets and pillowcases are for protecting my hair.

Lastly, thank you to my therapist mentor who taught me everything I know and to Chico and Heidi, who will now forever argue which of them I am referring to here.

appendix 1

My examples for finding the function of my care tasks:

Floors

1. Health and Safety: I need to remove tripping hazards and prevent bugs, mold, and bacteria from spreading or growing.
2. Comfort: I want room for kids to play; I don't like bits of dirt sticking to my feet when I am barefoot.
3. Happiness: I like the way the room looks when the floors are clean and mopped. Feels peaceful.

Laundry

1. Health and Safety: I need to have clean clothes to wear.
2. Comfort: I want my clothes to look nice and for me to find what I am looking for easily.
3. Happiness: I like having an aesthetically pleasing closet.

Tidying

1. Health and Safety: I need to remove tripping hazards.
2. Comfort: I want to be able to find the things I need, to have room for my hobbies, so my kids can focus better when they play.
3. Happiness: I like to be able to decorate for the holidays in the main room and it looks nicer to me if things are tidy. I like to create an inviting environment for guests.

Bathroom Cleaning

1. Health and Safety: I need to prevent mold and bacteria from growing or spreading.
2. Comfort: I want be able to find my things, to see clearly in the mirror, for things to smell good.
3. Happiness: I like to have a calming place to take a bath; I like to have a clear spot to do my makeup.

Dishes

1. Health and Safety: I need to have clean dishes with which to eat and cook.
2. Comfort: I want to have a clear sink to bathe the baby, to have more counter space available.
3. Happiness: I don't have a happiness layer for dishes.

Bathing/Showering

1. Health and Safety: I need to remove dirt and dead skin cells from my body.
2. Comfort: I want to have clean hair so I can look nice and not feel greasy. To smell nice and feel confident in public.
3. Happiness: I like to be able to relax, to focus on myself, and to read a book in the tub.

Dusting

1. Health and Safety: I need to prevent allergies and help control my asthma.
2. Comfort: I want to be able to set things down without them getting dusty, to remove pet fur so it doesn't get on my clothes.
3. Happiness: I like feeling like I have created a warm and inviting space for guests.

Cleaning My Kitchen

1. Health and Safety: I need to prevent bugs, bacteria, and mold from spreading or growing.
2. Comfort: I want to have plenty of space to cook and do my hobbies on the kitchen island. It's easy to sit down for family dinner when the table is clear.
3. Happiness: I like the way my kitchen looks when the counters are clear.

The key to finding a system that works for you is (1) understanding the function of the care task, (2) realizing there is no "right" way, only the right way for your family, and (3) creating a system around your habits (not habits around your system). For those reasons, the only person who can tell you what system is right for you is you. Below I'll share with you some ideas and questions to get you thinking. Remember, it takes time to find what works!

laundry

Family closet: Many families with small children elect to put everyone's clothes in the same big closet (or room). This makes dressing everyone in the morning easier, putting away laundry faster (since it all goes into one location), and usually centralizes where the dirty laundry ends up. Bonus points if you can place this location near the washer and dryer.

No-fold baskets: How much of your laundry really needs to be folded? Certainly not underwear, pajamas, or athletic shorts. How much stress and time could you save if you instead sorted unfolded laundry into baskets? If you do other people's laundry, can you sort into personalized baskets and allow them to fend for themselves for folding?

Hang it all: Some people find that hanging everything straight from the dryer is a more manageable system. Hanging makes it easier to see everything and arguably takes less time than folding. No room in the closet to hang everything? You can hang it anywhere, like on a rack in your bedroom.

Category washing: If you washed loads by person or by type of clothing you wouldn't have to spend time sorting. Taking that time or hassle off the task can make all the difference for some people

Explore different rhythms: For some people, washing a small load every day is more manageable. For others, having a designated washday is preferable since they don't have to think about laundry but once a week.

Downsize: Having less clothes might be the answer for your laundry woes. If you had fewer clothes on hand laundry loads would be smaller. However, if you missed a day you might end up with no clean underwear!

Color palette wardrobe: One way to downsize your closet (and therefore your laundry) without sacrificing the number of outfits you have is to do a color palette wardrobe. By picking up four to six complementary colors you can ensure that fewer pieces can make more outfits. Bonus points that the stress of dressing is cut down because everything goes with everything.

Outsource it: Can you afford a wash and fold or for someone to come and do your laundry? If laundry is really your bugbear, why not outsource it completely and move on with your awesome life?

dishes

Closing duties: Making daily dishes a part of your closing duties allows you to do a manageable load every day without having to try to "keep up" all day long.

Lighter dishes: If you have energy or mobility limitations, switching heavy glass dishes out for light plastic dishes can make the task of doing dishes less draining. Even mentally, lighter dishes can make the task feel less burdensome.

One dish per person: Some families have luck assigning each person one cup, plate, and bowl (sometimes color coded). Those old enough are responsible for their own dishes and the limited amount means you never end up with an overwhelming sink full of dishes.

Right into the dishwasher: If you have a dishwasher, consider taking the time to unload your dishwasher first thing in the morning (perhaps even getting up a little earlier to do so). That way, every dish that is dirtied can be placed straight into the dishwasher.

Paper plates: If you have barriers that make doing your dishes a serious impediment to your quality of life, consider switching to paper plates, even if just for a season. Postpartum, bereavement, depressive episodes, and health problems are seasons that require all of your energy and attention.

Dirty-dish station: Getting a drying rack just for dirty dishes can mean that when it comes time to wash them or load them into the dishwasher you feel less overwhelmed. This is because the dishes are organized in a way that is not visually overwhelming. Some families find that purchasing a dish tub really increases the functionality of their space. This way, dirty dishes can be placed into the tub, keeping the sink clear for other needs.

Extra silverware rack: I found that fishing the dirty silverware out of a gross sink was a huge sticking point for me. I bought a second dishwasher dish caddy and put it on the counter so I can throw dirty utensils in it all day and then just switch it out with the clean one at the end of the day!

Category washing: If your stage of life is such that dishes just seem to pile up, taking the time to place your dishes into categories before washing can help with feeling overwhelmed.

storage and organization

Baskets: Often the difference between messy and organized is a well-placed basket. The key is to put the basket where you are already making messes. Shoe pile by the front door? Basket. Laundry on the stairs? Basket. Trash on your nightstand? (Trash) basket.

Vertical junk drawer: If you have junk drawers or bins, a clear hanging shoe rack on the wall or back of a door can ensure you always have a place for small items and that you can see them all easily.

Visual storage: Some people love to see clear surfaces and open rooms. But not everyone cares for that aesthetic or needs that type of function. If you wish to have your items visible, you can design your own storage systems around that. Clear bins, 3M hooks on walls, trays, and extra open shelves are all ways to give each item a place and keep it out for ease of use and memory.

Trays: There are currently forty items sitting on my kitchen island. Yet it looks tidy because those items are compiled onto a large decorative lazy Susan, in a glass fruit bowl, in a cloth basket of baby snacks, and on four "to-do" trays. Even with the containers there is plenty of open space giving function for all things cooking, hobbying, and working.

Closets do not have rules: I once realized my hallway closet was a bit of a one-way street. I was always putting (and eventually cramming) things in, including coats, but almost never taking anything out. I had a hard time remembering what was in it and so mounted a bar of hooks on the outside to hold one jacket and one raincoat per family member. After realizing the one downstairs closet was a silly place to hold items almost never accessed, I relocated all the inside items to an upstairs closet, installed shelves, and used it instead for storing items previously cluttering up the kitchen and living room. Closets have no rules, you see. Do you have a closet that could better serve you?

Labels: As beautiful as custom-printed labels and bins are, often the pursuit of aesthetic perfection holds back real functional improvements. Post-it notes or masking tape does just fine and putting a label even on a piece of shelf denoting an item's permanent "home" can be helpful when tidying.

Papers and mail: Important papers are often easiest to store in an accordion file. If you struggle with mail upkeep, a visual system may be helpful: writing the due date and hanging a bill from the fridge or a corkboard. Some like to scan and save sentimental items, then throw away the physical copies.

about the author

KC Davis is a licensed professional therapist, author, and speaker. She is the creator of the mental health platform Struggle Care, where she shares a revolutionary approach to self and home care for those dealing with mental health, physical illness, and hard seasons of life. KC began her mental health journey at sixteen, when she entered treatment for drug addiction and mental health issues. After getting sober, she became a speaker and advocate for mental health and recovery. Professionally, KC has worked most of her career in the field of addiction in roles such a therapist, consultant, and executive director. She lives in Houston with her husband and two daughters.